Through the Vermilion Gates
A Journey Into China's Past

Through the Vermilion Gates

A Journey Into China's Past

ELEANOR C. MUNRO

Pantheon Books

Grateful acknowledgment is made for the use of the illustrations: The Art Institute of Chicago, S. M. Wickerson Collection: page 20–21A. Art News, Incorporated: page 96–97B. Center of Asian Art and Culture, The Avery Brundage Collection, San Francisco, California: page 2. The Cleveland Museum of Art: page 49A, Gift of Mr. and Mrs. Ralph King; page 49B, Gift of Harold T. Clark in memory of Flora L. Terry; page 80A, Purchase from the J. H. Wade Fund; page 100–101B, Mr. and Mrs. Severance A. Millikin Collection; page 122–123, Gift of the Hanna Fund. City Art Museum of St. Louis, Samuel C. Davis Collection: page 131B. Photo by C. Arthaud and F. Herbert-Stevens, from *L'Art de la Chine*, Editions Arthaud: page 14–15. The Fogg Art Museum, Harvard University: page 20–21E. The Institute of History and Philology, Academia Sinica, Republic of China: page 28–29; page 34C. Los Angeles County Museum of Art, Los Angeles County Funds: page 131A. The Metropolitan Museum of Art: page 20–21C, Rogers Fund, 1922; page 20–21D, Rogers Fund, 1943; page 34A, Rogers Fund, 1943; page 34B, Kennedy Fund, 1913; page 46, Rogers Fund, 1951; page 80C, Fletcher Fund, 1926; page 83A, Kennedy Fund, 1913; page 83B, Rogers Fund, 1925; page 100–101A, Gift of Arthur M. Sackler in honor of his parents, Isaac and Sophia Sackler, 1965; page 100–101C, Fletcher Fund, 1940; page 120, Fletcher Fund, 1928; page 131C, Gift of Robert E. Tod, 1937. The Minneapolis Institute of Arts: page 80B. Museum of Fine Arts, Boston: page 86–87A,B; page 96–97A, Ross Collection. Nelson Gallery—Atkins Museum, Kansas City, Missouri (Nelson Fund): page 125; page 132; cover. Philadelphia Museum of Art: page 39, Given by Horace H. F. Jayne; page 79B, Given by Charles H. Ludington. Portland Art Museum, Portland, Oregon: page 83C. The University Museum, University of Pennsylvania: page 76. Wadsworth Atheneum, Hartford, Connecticut: page 79A. Yale University Art Gallery: page 20–21B. Mr. and Mrs. Eugene Bernat: page 48, photograph by Lee Boltin.

TO DAVID AND LEXY

adventurers into the future

Acknowledgments

Some books which present additional material in a simple way are listed in the Further Reading List at the end of this volume. However there are some sources which older readers may wish to consult and to which I am grateful for permission to quote.

These include: Bingham, Woodbridge. *Founding of the T'ang Dynasty* (Waverly Press, Baltimore. 1941); Cheng Te-k'un. *New Light on Prehistoric China* (Cambridge University Press, London. 1966); Creel, Herrlee Glessner. *Birth of China* (Jonathan Cape, London. 1936); Fitzgerald, C. P. *China, a Short Cultural History* (Praeger, New York. 1958), *Chinese View of their Place in the World* (Oxford University Press, London. 1964), *Empress Wu* (Cresset Press, London. 1968), *Son of Heaven, Li Shih Min* (Cambridge University Press, London. 1933); Granet, Marcel. *Chinese Civilization* (Meridian, New York. 1958); Ho, Wai-kam. "Notes on two Chinese Sculptures from Northern Ch'i to Sui" in *Archives of Asian Art,* Vol. XXII, 1968–9; Honour, Hugh. *Chinoiserie, The Vision of Cathay* (John Murray, London. 1961); Hudson, G. F. *Europe and China* (E. Arnold, London. 1931); Munro, Donald J. *The Concept of Man in Early China* (Stanford University Press, Stanford. 1969); Pulleyblank, Edwin G. *An Lu Shan Rebellion* (Oxford University Press, London. 1955); Sickman, Laurence and Alexander Soper. *Art and Architecture of China* (Penguin, New York); Sirén, Osvald. *Chinese on the Art of Painting* (Schocken, New York. 1963); Sitwell, Sachaverell. *Touching the Orient* (Duckworth, London. 1934); *Sources of Chinese Tradition,* William T. deBary, ed. (Columbia University Press, New York. 1960); Twitchett, Denis. *Land Tenure and the Social Order in T'ang and Sung China* (Oxford University Press, London. 1962); Waley, Arthur. *Three Ways of Thought in Ancient China* (Doubleday, New York. 1956); Wright, Arthur F. "Buddhism and Chinese Culture" in *Journal of Asian Studies,* Vol. XVII, *Confucian Personalities* (Stanford University Press, Stanford. 1962), *The Confucian Persuasion,* ed. with Denis Twitchett (Stanford University Press, Stanford. 1960), "Symbolism and Function. Reflections of Ch'ang-an and other Great Cities" in *Journal of Asian Studies,* Vol. XXIV No. 4, August 1965, "T'ang Tai Tsung and Buddhism" (unpublished paper prepared for the Conference on T'ang Studies, Sydney Sussex College, Cambridge, 1969).

Grateful acknowledgment is made for permission to reprint from the following: *The Jade Mountain,* translated by Witter Bynner. Copyright 1929 and renewed 1957 by Alfred A. Knopf, Inc. Reprinted by permission of the publisher. (Pages 7, 102 bottom, 107, 108, 109 bottom, 116.) *Birth of China,* by H. G. Creel. Copyright 1936. Reprinted by permission of Curtis Brown, Ltd. (Pages 23, 30.) *Sources of Chinese Tradition,* edited by William T. de Bary. Copyright 1960. Reprinted by permission of Columbia University Press. (Page 36.) *The White Pony,* edited by Robert Payne. John Day Company, 1947. Reprinted by permission of Robert Payne. (Pages 74, 91.) *Cities of Destiny,* edited by A. Toynbee. Copyright 1967. Used by permission of McGraw-Hill Book Company. (Page 84.) *Chinese Civilization,* by Marcel Granet. Copyright 1958. Reprinted by permission of Routledge and Kegan Paul, Ltd. (Pages 99, 102 top.) *From the Chinese,* edited by R. C. Trevelyan. Copyright 1945. Reprinted by permission of George Allen and Unwin, Ltd. (Page 104.) *The Poetry and Career of Li Po,* by Arthur Waley. Copyright 1950. Reprinted by permission of George Allen and Unwin, Ltd. (Page 109.)

Chinese scholarship today is a field of adventure and some contradiction. Professor Arthur F. Wright of Yale generously gave me guidance and warning about pitfalls, and I have drawn much from his writings on the T'ang period. Various sections of this book are based on the works of scholars like the late Arthur Waley, and Professor Reischauer of Harvard, whose books on Hsüan-tsang, the poets, and Ennin I quote from. *Europe and China* by G. F. Hudson is a fascinating account of intersecting civilizations, source for my discussion of that subject; and Professor Pulleyblank's work on the An Lu-shan Rebellion was the source for my account of that episode. From Wai-kam Ho's "Notes on two Chinese Sculptures" I have taken, while somewhat rephrasing, an inscription. And particularly to Professor Schafer, whose rich volumes on the material treasures of the T'ang world provided the basis for my treatment of it, I am indebted.

Professor Chang Chun-shu, in particular, and Professor Donald J. Munro of the University of Michigan, and Robert M. Somers of Yale, read the manuscript and made crucial suggestions. Professor James C. Thomson gave me welcome advice about translation.

Professor Li Chi of the Academia Sinica in Taipei recreated for me during a long morning's conversation there the exhilaration of his early days digging at Anyang. Later he told the true sequence of events leading to the solution of the "dragons' bones" mystery and allowed me to see the photographs, documents and relics of those days in his possession.

I should not like to suggest, however, that any swamps I have stumbled into are due to misdirection on the part of these generous scholars. Missteps, obviously, are my own. Much of the pleasure of this adventure, I should add, came from the encouragement and company of my husband, E. J. Kahn Jr.

Contents

List of Illustrations

Through the Vermilion Gates
A Journey Into China's Past

Prologue

There are two—or perhaps a thousand trillion, as the Chinese storyteller would say—Chinas. One is the contradictory and still incompletely known China of historical fact. The other is the China of men's imagining—a land of blue-green porcelain pagodas, kingdom of peace and harmony where all men live together in the shade of their Wise Ancestors. There is a blacker side to this imaginary view of China, too. According to this position, which was that of some nineteenth century Americans, China is the Kingdom of Darkness, where Beelzebub rules his heathen millions.

Between these and other untruths about China, Westerners have shifted since the time of the Greeks, when rumors of a land "beyond the North Wind" first began to be heard. Only in our own century, with the tools of modern archaeology at hand, have scholars set out to rediscover the facts about its more than three thousand years of history. This is the story of the search back to one of the most dramatic and brilliant epochs of China's past: the T'ang Dynasty.

The T'ang Dynasty, which lasted from 618 until 907, coincided with the western Dark Ages. Earlier, in both West and East, at about the same time, the first "classic" civilizations of Graeco-Rome and Han China had fallen to tribes of warriors welling up in wave after wave from the Central Asian steppes. When Charlemagne knelt in St. Peter's basilica in Rome in the year 800, to take on the crown of the Holy Roman Empire, he wanted to erect on the ruins of the western classic world a new one, rooted to be sure in Rome but reinvigorated by his own Christianized tribal spirit. The T'ang Dynasty also was founded upon ruins by swashbuckling empire-builders as ambitious as Charlemagne. By the year 800, the Dynasty had passed its zenith, but it had still a century to endure. The forms of its society still seemed fresh and full of potential. The arts of the time were robust and equally full of promise of future sophistication. And the T'ang rulers themselves were, we can see behind their stiff formal portraits, human beings given to the passions and fears of all men and to a curiosity about the outside world not often equalled in China later on.

We know of course that Charlemagne's program was premature. His empire collapsed. Not until Gothic and then Renaissance Europe coalesced out of the medieval turmoil was his dream of a new Rome to be realized, and then it was a splintered empire indeed, where ideas about government, the arts, commerce and the rights of men fermented in many different "nations" divided by their languages and national boundaries.

In China, however, this splitting apart of a continent into many parts did not occur. There were always, to be sure, some deep differences between the people of the North and those of the South, between men of the mountains and those of the plains. But in the main, China's people were bound together by their common written language and their powerfully uniting religions. When invasions of foreigners occurred and native dynasties like the Han, the T'ang and later ones gave up the ghost, the Chinese drew into themselves and bided their time, knowing that sooner or later their superior civilization would conquer the conquerors and the unified Empire would be reborn. In this way, though many rulers were overthrown, still certain fundamental attitudes about men's life and the Empire as a historical whole have prevailed through China's lifetime. So to arrive at an under-standing of any single Chinese dynasty, it is well to travel through the gates of the earlier ones on which it was built, and once there, one can see clear lines of development toward future ones.

Unfortunately, however, within the million and more square miles of

China, almost no large-scale monuments remain of the ancient and medieval cities. Scholars have learned of Assyria's savagery in the lion hunt and war, and Rome's political ambitions, and Byzantium's transcendent faith from the ruins of their architecture. But of T'ang Ch'ang-an, for instance—one of the two greatest cities in the world at the time—only two ruined pagodas are standing today. Light wood pillars and pounded earth walls were all the architects needed to create their ambience of splendor and seeming permanence, and if, within a generation, the rain and wars swept them away, then new palaces and pavilions could be erected later on, upon the old foundations, according to formulae written in the books each dynasty kept to hand down to the next.

So instead of to monumental ruins of aqueducts and temples, students of the Chinese past must turn, for one thing, to a snowdrift of small objects which are buried underground: bits of engraved bone and tortoise shell—"dragons' bones," which tell a fascinating story; engraved bronze vessels of people flourishing while Tutenkamen reigned in Egypt; and, from the T'ang era itself, figurines of clay which were put into graves, showing T'ang men and women going about their daily business—musicians playing pipes and drums, dancers lifting their long sleeves, actors and jugglers, and animals which could be seen in the streets of Ch'ang-an, like horses and camels and an occasional elephant.

Also, during the many centuries when Buddhism held China in thrall, temples were carved out of rocky cliffs and filled with stone and stucco statues which survived the ages. From the ruins of these we can tell a good deal about the style of life before and during the T'ang Dynasty, when the greatest shrines were made.

Beyond these tangible relics of the past are the richly informative but confusing written histories of fallen dynasties. Each ruler of China had a staff of historians whose task it was to interpret their sovereign's acts in the light of an overriding theory: that in the Central Kingdom, only the Just ruled—that the Mandate of Heaven was a kind of mystic sign passed from the divine powers to the hand of the sole mortal deserving of it. So, in the dynastic histories lie seeds of historic truth, but buried under such embroidery and propaganda, such superimposed moral judgments, that sorting out truth from fiction is a major problem confronting modern China scholars.

And in fact even once the distortions are corrected, the histories tell only a partial story, for from our point of view some vital themes are neglected: the peasants, for instance, who always played a crucial role by carrying foward the primitive routine of the rice paddies, were hardly considered worth discussing. Nor was the merchant's influence on society considered important—his efforts to break out of old patterns, to reach far-off markets— for according to Confucian standards he was an individual near the bottom of the social scale without historic relevance.

Thus, in piecing together a picture of a long-past Chinese dynasty, major problems exist. Among these, perhaps the most nagging is that contradiction underlies nearly every aspect of Chinese life. There is almost nothing that can be said of China to which it is not necessary to add "Though, on the other hand . . ." Negligence of human life, for instance, which seems barbaric to us today, involving human sacrifice and slavery, went hand in hand with kindness; down-to-earth reasonableness with belief in supernatural powers; artful invention in some areas with a lack of curiosity in others. Swift, ruthless punishment was levied on enemies of the Dragon Throne: spies were boiled in oil; grave robbers were sliced into thin pieces. Yet T'ang judges, like their colleagues through Chinese history, were closely supervised from a central bureau; they were forbidden to drink wine while sitting in judgment, and they tried hard to avoid imposing the death penalty on ordinary transgressors. There is scant evidence of scientific method being applied to problems of daily life which forced mechanical inventions in the West; yet the compass, gunpowder and moveable type were first made in Asia. There was little systematic research in medicine, engineering or other sciences which absorbed Western artists and scholars from the monastic days onward. Instead, sorcerers plied their trade offering Elixirs of Immortality, and the gods of river, wind and rain were invoked against drought and flood. Yet more than in Europe, the humanistic virtues of tolerance and charity were practiced and the hungry poor of all intellectual beliefs could be comforted in Buddhist temples.

All these and other attitudes act as templates—as the modern biologist would say—against which the paradoxical attitudes of modern China have been shaped. Which is one, but not the only, reason for learning about the T'ang Dynasty. Another is to re-live a period when, like today, optimism conflicted in men's minds with their sense of overhanging danger, and poets, while lamenting their land worn out by battle, still had the heart to enjoy their "countryside blue and still after the long rain."

Chapter 1 Into the Desert

Rough were the mountain-stones and the path very narrow;
And when I reached the temples, bats were in the dusk . . .
On the old wall, said the priest, were Buddhas, finely painted.
And he brought a light and showed me, and I called them wonderful . . .

(HAN YU)

For seventeen days, the Englishman had spurred his horse across a wash of dry gravel which seemed to have no end. He was, he felt, truly near the "Roof of the World," for he had left behind the mountains bearing that name—the Pamirs, that guard the border between northwest India and Chinese Turkestan—only eleven months before, not long as the traveler here must clock time. In April of 1906, Aurel Stein, with a Chinese translator and aide and a caravan of porters, had left Kashmir. Now it was March of the following year, and he was only just drawing close to his destination, riding straight into the teeth of "cutting east winds, the very home of which we now seemed to approach!"

7

On the map, the territory Stein was crossing looks endless indeed. The route leads from the Pamirs to the basin of the Tarim River and thence to the little relic of lake which lies in the desolate salt flats of Lop Nor. Here, Stein had come six years earlier to explore the traces of a ruined wall that, around the time of Christ, protected the mighty Han Empire of China from the attacks of its enemies.

Here and there in the sand, Stein had found objects of great interest and value: not gold or silver, but short, flat planks of wood, some still tied together in bundles, bearing ragged Chinese characters in black ink. These were ancient letters and official documents, written by and to soldiers posted in this remote outland two millenia ago. Removed from their families and the landscape of fertile plains they had known, lonely in their garrisons, these men had taken time from currying their horses and polishing their swords to write memos, keep inventories, tally up their accounts. Some were urgent messages. "With long lungs make haste!" one letter implored. Perhaps an enemy warrior was closing in at the very instant the soldier picked up his brush to call for help.

On that first trip, at the season of "burans," or windstorms, Stein had also spent some time digging in the gritty earth near the ancient trading-post of Khotan. Under his supervision, men from the village removed the sand of centuries from a series of ruined walls. Within, Stein discovered a sizeable temple decorated with stucco statues. The form of these sculptures said much to Stein about the exchange of artistic ideas between West and East, for the figures were cloaked in Roman togas but set in the pose of the Indian god Buddha.

Stein photographed the figures and would have liked to take them back to the British Museum in London which was partly responsible for his expedition. But they were so fragile after two thousand windy years that they crumbled at the touch. So before continuing his march, Stein covered them up again with sand. "It was a melancholy duty to perform," he later wrote in his journal, "strangely reminding me of a true burial . . . images I had brought to light, vanishing again one after the other, under the pall of sand which had hidden them for so many centuries."

Other objects he found in the sand here were also full of meaning to the knowledgeable traveler. One was a Greek coin stamped with a graceful little figure of Eros lifting his wings. When Stein found this coin beside his boot, he had positive proof that, two thousand years earlier, an exchange had taken place in that very spot between men of the West, the Greeks, and agents of the eastward-lying lands which touched the Central Kingdom, then only dimly known to the Greeks as the land of the mysterious Hyperboreans.

Another route leads eastward from the Pamirs, passing through Khotan and then reaching Cherchen, another trade-post. Beyond, it swings through An-hsi and, finally, descends southeast to the modern city of Sian. A traveler this way during the T'ang Dynasty would now have arrived at the towering, pounded earth and tiled walls of the greatest city in the world, China's capital, Ch'ang-an, first eastern terminus of the silk route. At the western end, highways branched off toward markets at different points as history raised up and then demolished great cities: Samarkand was a rich waystop, Constantinople lay to the north, Alexandria to the south. When Ch'ang-an flourished, Rome lay in ruins, but for centuries before it had been Urbs in Orbis, City at the Hub of the Universe, ultimate market-place of the western world.

Across the unimaginable miles of mountains and deserts of this highway, information was passed back and forth even in ancient times between camel drivers and nomad warriors. These garbled tales were full of error and fancy, yet they contained ghosts of the truth about the two great civilizations of East and West. Aurel Stein's dream had been to explore the very midpoint of this highway, the place where gossip and imagination had bred upon truth. There, at the world's roof, he was convinced that some of the most exciting and important events of man's history had taken place. He wished to reconstruct those events from clues all but obliterated by the winds which ceaselessly pour out of the Mongolian uplands, across the Gobi Desert and the sands of Takla Makan.

Now, on his second expedition, Stein was coming close to the most famous intersection on the old trade route: the oasis town of Tun-huang, branching point for the north and south highways which linked China, India, Mongolia and the West. It is a town whose dilating fortunes have reflected history, for whenever China was strong, Tun-huang lay within her grasp, but when barbarian enemies ruled the marches, Tun-huang was abandoned. Here Stein hoped to uncover tangible evidence of this crossroads in history, when China reached westward, and the West replied.

9

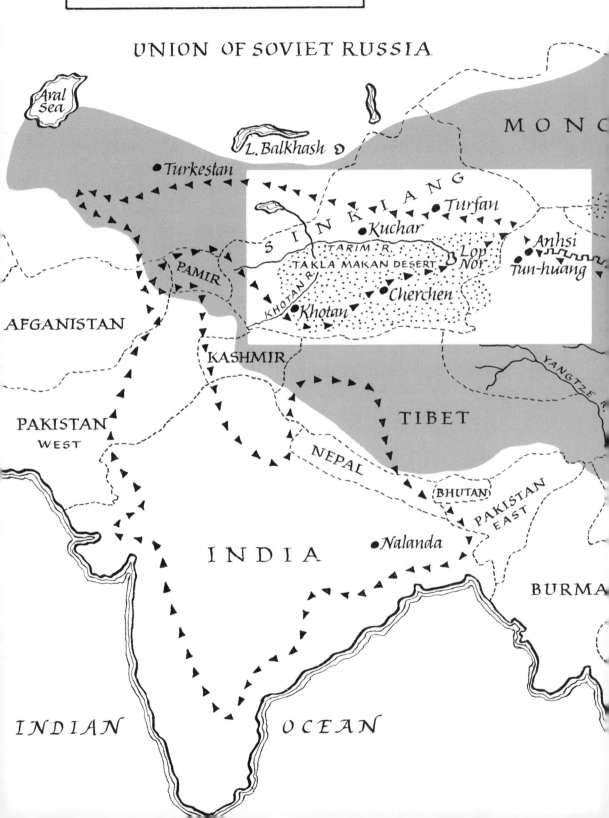

Sites mentioned in book
appear on this map

UNION OF SOVIET RUSSIA

Aral
Sea

MONG

L. Balkhash

•Turkestan

SINKIANG

Turfan

Kuchar

TARIM R.

TAKLA MAKAN DESERT

Lop
Nor

Anhsi

Tun-huang

KHOTAN R.

Cherchen

PAMIR

Khotan

AFGANISTAN

KASHMIR

YANGTZE

PAKISTAN
WEST

TIBET

NEPAL

PAKISTAN

BHUTAN

EAST

INDIA

Nalanda

BURMA

INDIAN   OCEAN

Lake
Baykal

SEA OF
JAPAN

KOREA

I A

MONGOLIA

INNER

BI
SERT

Peking

HOPEH

Anyang

YELLOW
SEA

PACIFIC

OCEAN

YELLOW R.

YELLOW R.

YELLOW R.

WEI

Loyang
Chang-an Lung-men caves
(Modern Sian)

Suchou

Kyoto
Nara

J A P A N

YANGTZE R.

C H I N A

TAIWAN

Canton

MILES

0   200   400   600   800   1000

HAINAN

LAOS

AILAND

CAMBODIA

VIETNAM

SOUTH CHINA SEA

Extent of Tang Empire ca. 700 A.D.

◄◄◄ Route of Hsüan-tsang

☐ Area of Aurel Stein's explorations

---- Modern Boundaries

�519ᴝ The Great Wall of China

Ascherl

Stein had plotted his route across the frightening desert of Takla Makan. "You see nothing but sky and sands . . . the bones of men and beasts, and droppings of camels," wrote one early Chinese traveler. "You hear sounds of ringing, or wailing . . . these are the voices of spirits and goblins." We would say, rather, that rocks in the desert form wind-chambers giving out minor-keyed wailing noises. But early travelers were sure these sounds were the voices of demons, beckoning them off the path to sure death in the waterless sands. "Such are the troubles and dangers in the desert of Lop Nor," on the road to Tun-huang, reported Marco Polo, who came this way in the thirteenth century.

Before setting out, Stein had prepared himself for all eventualities by adding two carpenters, a blacksmith and a leatherworker to his caravan. In these remote regions, it might be that no stranger would come forward to supply these services. And yet, generosity flourished even in the desert, where men must assist one another or die. One night, exhausted at the end of a long march, Stein found a gourd of milk and a basket of fresh eggs beside his tent, left by some passing nomad. By torchlight, he feasted on these and on dried meat and fruit.

Another night, protected from the icy wind which rattled his tent, Stein peered out to see a caravan of fifty camels lumber swiftly by, loaded with bales of tea from Tun-huang. The driver refused Stein's invitation to stop for refreshment. He too was in a hurry to end the dangerous passage. "Like some phantom," Stein wrote in his journal, the line of camels passed by, its "tinkling train" no different from caravans of the Han Dynasty.

Eventually the desert was left behind. In December, Stein began to turn up scraps of wool carpet along the way, and bits of yellowed silk, fragments of bronze, lacquer, glass and copper coins. Finally, after traversing the long stretch of gravel, he caught sight of a distant line of feathery trees and green fields. Slowly, Tun-huang, "City of Sands" rose up against the sky.

The town was enclosed in square mud-brick and pounded-earth walls. A ruined gate admitted Stein and his weary train. The town itself was a disappointment, shabby and desolate. Where once upon a time rich bazaars had offered the sophisticated wares of the world, now cheap manufactured items from Russia, Britain and China were spread out in the dusty streets for the casual buyer. In the age of ocean freighters and transcontinental railroads, Tun-huang was as far off the main route as a village grocery store.

Stein made arrangements to pitch his tent in a peach orchard and to billet his men in the cavernous rooms of a nearby rich man's dwelling. Then he introduced himself to the governors of the town, mild-mannered, smooth-faced gentlemen in thick quilted coats, who were eager to show him hospitality. But wherever he turned, he seemed to see clearly before his eyes the face of another traveler, from long-ago China, whose every footstep Stein had committed to memory and who, more than anyone else, had lured him away from the comforts of London: "My saintly guide and patron, Hsüan-tsang!"

Hsüan-tsang was a Buddhist monk who lived in the early years of the T'ang Dynasty. At a young age, he had set out from Ch'ang-an to travel to India in order to find out which of the thousandfold teachings of the Buddha then being bandied about in China were authentic. Eventually, Hsüan-tsang became as famous in China as King Arthur is in the West, and children were told and re-told his adventures by their parents and teachers to instill in them, too, the ideals of courage and self-sacrifice in following the truth.

Aurel Stein knew that when Hsüan-tsang made his way north, some four-teen hundred years earlier, Tun-huang had lain in ruins, for the northern marches had only just been reclaimed from barbarian tribes that had held power there since the fall of the Han Dynasty. So Hsüan did not visit the town itself, though he was advised to from the touristic point of view. Instead, he pushed straight on over the northern route through Turfan to India. After sixteen years there, he came back over the same ground. "Four marches after Niya, six after Cherchen . . ." he reported having passed near the ruins of "old towns, famous in Central Asian history." There was no doubt in Aurel Stein's mind that the most famous of these ruined old towns was Tun-huang.

All the same, Stein's ultimate goal lay not in the shabby modern town itself but outside its walls. There, some ten miles southeast, beyond a shelf of land covered, in March when he arrived, with a thin sheet of ice, a perpendicular ridge of cliffs jutted upward, and into these had been cut a honeycomb of cells and shrines which comprised a vast and living temple to the god Buddha. This cliff temple (overleaf) had been constructed over the course of centuries, but it enjoyed particular popularity during the T'ang Dynasty, when both the practice and teaching of Buddhism, and foreign trade, brought many pilgrims to these lonely regions.

Hardly able to contain his excitement, Stein rode out to these decorated caves, and once he was there, standing before this hive of ruined sculptures and flaking paintings, he "could not doubt for a moment that the best belonged to the times of the T'ang Dynasty." Before his eyes rose up, in steps to the sky, a painted carpet of Buddhist images. There were frescoes of dragons which leapt over the red walls beside fleet-footed horses, galloping like shreds of clouds. Cross-legged Buddhist sages sat on the backs of these beasts, raising their hands in dreamy blessing to the pilgrims below. There were scenes of the Buddhist paradise, ringed with blue mountains at whose crest angels and flowers danced in the breezes. There were rows upon rows of sculptures too, Buddhist saints and holy men dressed in Indian scarves and robes, and tooth-gnashing Guardians of the Four Directions, and the wrinkled forms of Ahrats, men who had mastered every point of Buddhist truth and were only awaiting their death to release them into Nirvana.

Setting to work, Stein photographed and took notes on all he saw so that he could make a report back to London. Then, because he had other tasks to finish in the desert before summer came, he left Tun-huang, little knowing that a discovery greater than all this awaited him on his return—one of the most exciting finds of modern archaeology, comparable in ways to the finding of the royal palaces at Ur, or the tombs of the Greek heroes at Mycenae.

For some weeks, hastening against the rising heat, Stein traced his way along the old Han wall he had already encountered. He came to a row of ruined watchtowers silently overlooking the desert, and a passing camel-driver informed him that they marked "the old Han road from An-hsi to Lop Nor." He discovered the ruins of the old Jade Gate, main station of this line of fortifications, and not far off, he gazed down into the somber blackness of a well which Han soldiers had dug for a dungeon. Nearby stood the ruins of a stone granary. And always underfoot, he found more Han letters, brushed in black ink on poplar or fir from the forests which then grew where now there was sand, and on bamboo, imported from groves in the south of China. "A barbarian horseman rides toward the watch station with a drawn bow," one reported. "Crossbows discharge. He retires." And one more soldier of the Han army was spared to pick up his brush and write. By now, Stein was on the very border of the "Great Gobi," where "the feeling of remoteness which the whole silent landscape breathed was shared even by the wild camels."

The temperature now scaled upward toward 150 degrees at midday, so Stein turned back toward Tun-huang. Leaving the sands where mirages danced, he marched back through fields now hazed over with iris and corn, back to his encampment in the peach orchard. Along the way, the elms of Tun-huang were now in heavy leaf, drawing nourishment from underground springs which had fed the oasis for millenia. Hardly pausing to rest and read the bags of mail that followed him wherever he camped, Stein rode back out to the "Cave of the Thousand Buddhas." Before leaving on this last trek, he had heard a rumor in the marketplace, and he was eager to find out whether it had any substance. A mysterious cache of manuscripts had been found in one of the caves, it was reported, and then walled up again at once, before anyone had had time to examine them.

Awaiting Stein at the cliff was a small man in long brown robes. He was a Taoist monk from the south of China who had settled down in these sacred premises to take care of them, hoping by his good works to earn a little merit in his climb to a heavenly reward. He spent his time, he explained, puttering around the temple cells, cleaning them of sand and dust and restoring the statues and wall paintings. Begging from door to door in Tun-huang he had managed to collect just enough money to keep himself alive and his project going.

Aurel Stein noted the man's eyes, "so shy and fitful," and realized that he would have to work hard to pry any secret from him. But at last, hesitantly, the little caretaker admitted that the rumor was true. He himself had made the interesting discovery some years earlier while shoveling a drift of sand out of one of the caves. He had noticed a break in the plaster behind one statue. Squinting through the crack, he could just make out a second chamber beyond. He broke down the wall and there he found a secret room, crammed from floor to ceiling with rolls of manuscripts and paintings on silk and paper. He had been astonished by this discovery, but he was, alas, no scholar himself, and so, rather than risk losing such holy relics to robbers or tourists, he had walled them up again, first with a stout wooden door and then with one of brick.

Stein contained his delight and curiosity and slowly set out to win the monk's confidence. He began by admiring the restorations he had made to the paintings and sculptures, overlooking the garish modern paints with which he had touched up the crumbling old forms. Some of the wall paintings showed Stein's "patron saint," Hsüan-tsang, in one or another of the many stories which had sprung up after his death: fighting a dragon, or snatched by a pack of demons, or patiently waiting for a turtle to ferry him across a river. But even as he studied these paintings, Stein was working persistently to convince his new friend to let him see the real treasures of the cave. What he wanted, of course, was to take them away from this remote spot, where they were in danger of being stolen or destroyed, to a great metropolitan museum where they could be properly studied.

Eventually Stein won his tug-of-war. The priest agreed to let him see the manuscripts, but only in secret. So one night, Stein waited in his tent until darkness had fallen and the porters had drifted off to sleep. Then he sent his Chinese secretary to climb up the cliff to the place of rendezvous. In pitch dark, the monk gave over the documents, and the secretary carried them back down to camp.

Once he had the documents in hand, Stein buckled the flap of his tent so no one could look in. Then he lit his kerosene lamp and hunched over his table. Eagerly he opened the scrolls. One after another, histories, religious writings, legends, stories and poems came into sight. Most, like the paintings and sculptures, dated from the T'ang Dynasty, China's medieval flowering, of which practically no trace had been thought still to exist. Apparently, the little caretaker had stumbled on the library of this important religious center, and just how international a place it had been was proved by the many languages in which the scrolls were written: Chinese, Sanskrit, Manichean, Sogdian, Uighur and others—all the tongues of the nomads who bordered these trails and of the high civilizations which the trails linked together.

But perhaps what most thrilled Stein, from a personal point of view, was finding several manuscripts with versions of the very scriptures brought home from India and then translated into Chinese by old Hsüan-tsang himself!

There were paintings too, on silk and on paper. These had lain crushed under the mountain of manuscripts, preserved like them in the dry rock hideaway. Eventually, when these had been cautiously unfolded, they turned out to be banners which had been held aloft during festival processions or hung in the temple cells. Often they had little weights at the bottom corners to make them flutter in the wind. Others had long side panels which must have writhed in the breeze like snakes.

Stein packed twenty-four cases of these treasures to be sent home to the British Museum. Later, a great French scholar, Paul Pelliot, followed his steps and took another group for his own country; and a final portion eventually went to the Indian government for safekeeping. Partly because of the disruptions of the past half-century of war, not all the manuscripts have been translated. But from those which have been, it is clear how rich T'ang literature was, both in abstruse religious writings and in lighthearted fairytales, poems, and stories.

And from studying the paintings in all their colorful detail, art historians have been able to piece together the fascinating story of how artistic ideas were carried back and forth across these trade routes. The subject that most engrossed these artists of the T'ang Dynasty was Buddhism. From Roman-trained artists in the West had come the idea of representing Buddha as a man-god, seated or standing tranquilly, with his muscular body swathed in the pleated robes of a Roman senator. From artists trained in the shops of India had come a swinging, tense line which traced his undulating body when it was represented in paint. And from Chinese artists came a wealth of fluttering and flying shapes—galloping horses, twisting ribbons, dragons, flowers and angels. Some paintings in Tun-huang showed the Buddhist paradise, a dream-land of lagoons and low hills with paths meandering through gardens. From these, one can imagine how the real gardens and pleasure pavilions of the T'ang aristocrats looked. Still other paintings showed processions of gay or solemn people, marching to the music of drums, flutes and finger-cymbals. These show us how T'ang people of the courts dressed and behaved, what music they liked, and how they worshipped. Even individual personalities pierced through the haze of time: one cave in the complex was dedicated by a rich princess of the westward-lying oasis city of Khotan; it showed women with elaborate headdresses, under a canopy of chrysanthemums.

One scroll contained a prayer to the Buddhist goddess of mercy, Kuan-yin, to send help against enemies which were, apparently, massing for the attack. Soon after the beginning of the tenth century, the keepers of this irreplaceable library must have recognized that danger threatened from tribes beginning to exercise their power as the great T'ang Empire collapsed. They must have prepared, secretly but well in advance, the rock-cut chamber in which the most precious of their possessions could be hidden. When the attack came, the librarians must have worked swiftly to stack their

A

B

C

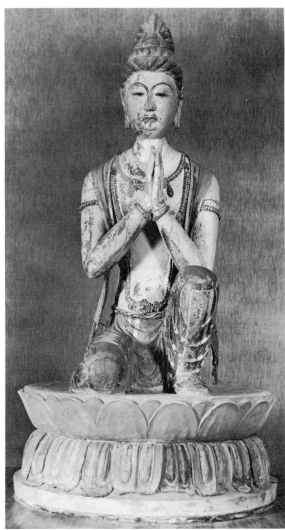

D   E

In the West, man's idea of the way Christ looked changed as centuries passed and different groups of people exercised their taste. For example, shortly after he died, Christ was shown as a young shepherd boy, in a loose toga, with a lamb on his shoulder; later, he was shown as a dark-eyed, bearded desert figure and, in the Renaissance, often as a mature but suffering human. So in the East, the image of the god Buddha underwent changes. At first, taught by Graeco-Roman artists near northwest India, sculptors showed him in classical, pleated robes, calmly seated or standing in natural poses (far left). At the top, is a scene of Buddha's mother giving birth as she lifts her hand to touch a tree. He leaps from her side into a cloth held by a servant. Next (near left), when northern peoples ruled China and tried to spread the foreign-born Buddhist faith, they made figures with a particular tense, nervous energy. T'ang artists were devout Buddhists; their figures of the god, by now absorbed into the Chinese pantheon, are solidly round, both human and deeply meditative (above left). At the top right is a painted clay figure of a Buddhist saint from the Tun-huang caves, kneeling on a lotus.

manuscripts, layer by layer, until the room was full. Perhaps they finished plastering over the wall just as enemy horses galloped up to the foot of the cliff. Thanks to their foresight, and to Aurel Stein's persistence, this rich and international moment in time has been preserved. Some modern scholars, looking backward, have criticized Stein for removing Chinese treasures to safekeeping in Britain. But, again in hindsight, considering the political disruptions which followed, one must at the least say that he acted with dedication to scholarship.

After he finished working at Tun-huang, Stein was still reluctant to say good-bye to this part of the world. He spent a last few months tracing "my wall" across the desert. He found other cliffs with cave-temples. He stood at the "Barrier of the Pleasant Valley," through which mounted patrols of the Han Dynasty had ridden out into enemy territory. Before him he could imagine the great body of China proper, with its mountains and rivers, its lush plains and its cities, and he asked himself which of the soldiers of old, passing through this gateway, could have been confident he would ever return again "within the walls," to his family and home.

Men of the Han Dynasty, which fell into ruin four centuries before the T'ang arose, were not the only ones who met their fate in these marches so near and yet so far from the Central Kingdom. Europeans too, later traveled this way. In the oasis town of Su-chou near the Great Wall, Stein came upon the lonely grave of a seventeenth-century Jesuit missionary, Benedict de Goes. The Jesuits who came East were, for the most part, learned men, full of curiosity about the land they knew as Cathay. "He sought Cathay," wrote one of de Goes' countrymen, "and found heaven."

Eventually Stein, who also sought Cathay, had also to admit failure in that respect, for since the Boxer Rebellion of 1900–1901, most foreigners were unwelcome in China. So Stein retraced his steps, back through the Takla Makan desert. On its western edge, he bade farewell to the camels who had made the treks with him. "Have they ever since wished to be back with their master," he wondered, " as I have often wished to travel again with them?"

A little later, he said good-bye to his Chinese friend and aide who had shared the adventure of Tun-huang. "As I rode on," he wrote later, in the travel-book on which his wider fame today rests, "the quivering glare and heat of the desert seemed to descend like a luminous curtain and hide from me the most cherished aspects of my Turkestan life."

Chapter 11 The Ancestral Temples

He called his superintendent of works
He called his minister of instruction
And charged them with the building of the house.
With the line, they made everything straight
They bound the frame boards tight . . .
Up rose the ancestral temple in its solemn grandeur . . .
(BOOK OF POETRY)

At the beginning of the twentieth century, when Aurel Stein was investigating the limits of the Han and the T'ang Dynasties in the deserts of Chinese Turkestan, almost nothing was known about the origins of Chinese civilization, from which these had evolved. In Europe, by contrast, artists and scholars had worked hard since the end of the Middle Ages to reconstruct past civilizations from the broken ruins which, they felt sure, held the key to understanding their own times. In the fifteenth century, for example, several sculptors and architects living in the city of Florence made a methodical study of the long-buried columns and carvings lying here and there, relics of Roman temples abandoned ever since the Germanic warriors had pillaged Italy a millenium before. In much the same way, men of the eighteenth century, including our own Thomas Jefferson, went back and studied Roman ruins—then coming to light in Pompeii—to formulate their own ideas about art, law and philosophy.

But with a few exceptions, almost no scientific archaeology had been carried out on Chinese soil. Ancient works of art in bronze or baked clay had always been deeply treasured by Chinese scholars for their perfume of long-gone ages. But these came onto the market only rarely and, because most of them had been stolen out of tombs by grave-robbers, they were almost never accompanied by hard facts about their place of origin. Thus, however much they were admired by their new owners, these works of art were of little value in trying to construct an accurate outline of Chinese history.

Almost everything that was known—or imagined to be known—about continuing Chinese history was contained in the written Standard Histories which each dynasty kept, and these, unfortunately, concealed the true facts in their own way, for each ruler naturally labored to have his reign remembered as a glorious one.

The ancient history of China, on the other hand, was presented in the so-called Book of History, assembled by Confucian scholars after the fifth century B.C. Here, much as in our Old Testament, legends about imaginary "First Ancestors" were mixed with bits of historical fact, fragments of old speeches and poems, and so forth.

The first ancestors, as some ancient classics suggested, had been half god, half man. There was Fu Hsi, with the body of a snake, who had taught the mountain people to fish with nets, to tame animals, to live together in families and to make music and write. There was Shen Nung, with the head of an ox. He had shown the people how to heal their wounds with herbs and to make rice and millet spring from their land. Huang Ti had shown them the secret of the wheel and how to protect their bodies with armor when they went to battle. Today, we know that these are myths of the kind all ancient peoples invented, unconsciously telling how their race gave up the first, rootless form of society and settled into the farming and fishing villages of the Late Stone Age.

But for what really happened in China before about 1122 B.C., when a people called "Chou" came into power around the bend of the Yellow

River, historians could find no solid evidence. The Chou were the first to keep careful written records, and some of these could be compared, for proof of their accuracy, with names of certain kings that were inscribed on a very few bronze vessels known to date from the Chou period. Yet there was much more in the written histories which applied to the millenia before—particularly descriptions of an earlier people called the Shang, who were said to have ruled that part of China for some six hundred years before it fell to the Chou.

One reason for this historical gap was, curiously, because Chinese peasants believed in ghosts. The airs were filled, they believed, with the invisible spirits of the dead, ready to revenge themselves on the man who disturbed their resting place either by accident or design. Many reasonable men had tried to speak out against this superstition. Confucius said the reason he mourned his mother after her death was just because then she was alive only in his mind. Later, a philosopher of the Han Dynasty mustered some scientific-sounding arguments against the idea: "Man lives because of his vital force," he reasoned, "and when he dies, this vital force is extinguished . . . the body decays and turns to clay. What is there to become a ghost then?" But the superstition would not die. As late as 1934, when a number of scientific expeditions had finally gotten underway, an official of the government petitioned the National Research Institute of History and Philology to stop the dig. Since grave robbers had always been punished in China by being sliced into pieces, why, he asked, were modern "robbers" being paid to insult the spirits in the name of science?

Nevertheless, around the turn of this century, a number of events coincided to force legend to wither away before science. The same had happened earlier in the case of western historical mysteries like Troy and Mycenae, great cities thought for a long time to have been only imaginary creations of poets.

The story goes that, one day, toward the end of the nineteenth century, just about the time Aurel Stein in London was getting ready to make his first expedition to Khotan, an elderly gentleman in Peking, one Mr. Wang, suffered an attack of malaria and sent to his herb doctor for a prescription to end his chills and fever. Mr. Wang was a cautious man, and before giving the herbs to his cook to boil into a broth, he decided to go over the ingredients item by item. Among them were some pieces considered a standard cure for malaria, and in fact for many other ailments of body and spirit—bits of bones and tortoise shell thought to be fossil remains of dragons. As Mr. Wang turned over these little objects, he thought he saw some lines engraved upon them. To his astonishment, when he studied them carefully, he saw they were marked with very ancient Chinese characters, somewhat like those which Chinese scholars had been accustomed to find upon bronze vessels of the Shang and the Chou periods.

Mr. Wang was an eminent statesman, a learned amateur of Chinese paleontology and a collector of bronzes. Fascinated by his discovery, he now set out to make a collection of shells which bore these curious inscriptions. However, as a scholar and friend of the West, he was attacked by the Boxer rebels, and lost his life in that uprising. His collection, which had grown to some three thousand examples, was left to his friend Mr. Liu, also a passionate amateur archaeologist, who eventually published six volumes reproducing these objects by means of ink squeezes.

At about the same time, in a village called Hsiao T'un in the district of Anyang, a farmer named Li noticed that after a rainstorm or at the season of his spring plowing, his fields became littered with mysterious, odd-shaped bits of bone. These, too, were faintly scratched with characters meaningless to farmer Li. He decided that the bits of bone which worked up through the sod of his fields must be the wonder-working dragons' bones, and he carried a number of them to apothecary shops in his village. No doubt other farmers were doing the same thing, for soon quite a business was going on in this merchandise, and some of the bones found their way to the bazaars of the big cities, where westerners and educated Chinese browsed. So it happened that, just about the time Mr. Wang fell ill, other scholars were coming across dragons' bones in the marketplace and beginning to wonder what they really were.

The Boxer Rebellion intervened, and the solving of the mystery had to be postponed. It was not until the early 'twenties that a number of scientists made their way to the source of the inscribed bones in Anyang and began to piece together the story of their origin and meaning. Meanwhile, a specialist on ancient China had published the fascinating news that the bones were marked with names and dates of certain kings also mentioned in the so far unprovable historical annals of the Shang!

The digs at Anyang were carried forward at first as a cooperative venture between the Chinese, represented by a brilliant young American-trained archaeologist named Li Chi, and the Freer Gallery of Art in Washington, D.C., which is part of the Smithsonian Institution. It was the dream of Li Chi, who is still at work in Taiwan, and his American colleague, Dr. Carl Whiting Williams, to break the barriers of suspicion which had for so long divided East and West and cooperate as scientists on this important work. But unfortunately there were disagreements, probably about the disposition of the finds since the United States was underwriting the dig. The Smithsonian withdrew its support, and for fifteen years, until the mid 1930s, the projects were continued on a shoestring by the Chinese alone.

The digging was tough. The plains of north China are covered with a deep layer of loose yellow soil called "loess." When the workers stooped over their shovels trying to sink exploratory pits into the ground, wind picked up the loess and flung it into their eyes. At their backs, they knew, bandits were stationed in their hideouts ready to shoot if a grave with bronze or gold objects turned up.

At first, however, only scraps of bones came into view. These were interesting, of course, but the scientists were after a bigger goal: to prove that the Shang people had really existed by finding the ruins of one of their cities. Eventually the Nationalist Government sent financial support and also some armed guards. And at last, by the mid 1930s, the archaeologists were successful, and a new level of history lay exposed for all the world to see.

By then, four royal Shang tombs had been found and completely excavated. These were no crude Stone Age pits in the earth, but colossal trenches shaped like pyramids turned on their tops (see next page). Mighty ramps led forty feet down into the subterranean burial place. Here, in fantastic array, lay the skeletons of men and women beheaded to serve their king in the spirit world. Horses too had collapsed where they were struck down or in grotesque heaps in a corner of the pit where they had tried to escape their executioners. Beside the horses, lay the bones of their grooms. There were even the ghostly traces of chariots ready to roll against a spirit-enemy, their bronze hub caps and leather reins still faintly visible. In one tomb were over six thousand objects of daily use—pottery vessels, carvings in shell, stone and bone, animal figures, and bronze shields, swords and crossbows. Faintly, the earth even preserved the wrinkled tracery of silk fabric long since rotted away.

Nearby lay the Great City of Shang, its walls, its palace, its common dwel-

ling places and roads. Laid out by the great Shang king, P'an Keng, the city had endured until its decline under the last Shang ruler, an ambitious figure who well deserved his defeat at the hand of a rebel. Or so the chronicles said. Soon thereafter, as if heaven decided to obliterate an unworthy race, the Great City had been inundated by a flood.

Thus, the richness and extent of the Shang Dynasty was at last brought to light, and it was clear that, as the histories had said, the classic forms of later Chinese society, philosophy, and architecture—for example, those of the T'ang Dynasty—derived much from patterns laid down here. Thus, to understand T'ang China, one must begin with the Great City Shang.

The city was built on a plain, well protected by the river before and mountains behind against what early men most feared: sudden attack by mounted enemies. The plain was well-watered, and abundantly stocked with animals for food and for the hunt.

> *Shu has gone hunting*
> *In his chariot and four.*
> *The reins are in his hands like ribbons*
> *The two outside horses prance . . .*

wrote a poet of this, the favorite sport of most Chinese emperors. One of them later was criticized by his own advisers for being fonder of chasing the stag, pheasant, and boar than he was of facing the affairs of his empire.

A great wall surrounded the city, made of earth dumped into a frame of wood and then pounded until it was hard. Dwellings in the Great City Shang were raised on platforms of pounded earth and roofed with reeds and wattle laid across rows of wooden columns. A rich man might paint his walls red or white; a poor man might live in what was little more than a pit in the earth flimsily covered with straw. Even in times of greatest prosperity, the Chinese city was never built like the pyramids of Egypt or the walls of Nineveh and Assur, in enduring stone. Earth and mud-brick seemed to suffice, along with columns hewn from cypress and pines which grew in the nearby hills.

Within the Great City Shang, tradesmen and artisans must have raised a busy clamor; jewelry makers and armorers plied their arts beside the workers in leather and bronze, while vendors of meat and grain called out their wares in the marketplace. But none of these were more vital to the life of the city than the farmers, whose fields lay between the city walls and the river. These providers of food, and the king who provided shelter and protection within his walls, were the two stable arms of early Chinese society.

There was no escape for the Chinese peasant from the most simple fact of his life: he needed the earth to feed him, and it needed him to bring it to flower. Thus, from his patient giving-in to the rhythm of the seasons, the dwindling and coming of the crops—wheat and millet in the north, rice in the south—the Chinese took a model for his behavior. Obedience to patterns of nature which could not be changed seemed more useful than originality or exciting independence. That man seemed wisest who most willingly accepted the pattern of life shared both by the straw-hatted tiller of the field, and the king, "First Farmer" of the land.

For the Chinese king was, from earliest times, more than simply a leader in battle. Upon his shoulders, as on the shoulders of the father of a family, rested responsibility for the smooth running of the entire universe, as well as for his kingdom. Unless he performed the proper sacrifices at the turning of the seasons, for instance, the fish would not awaken in the melting rivers of spring, the east wind not blow to thin the ice upon the fields. Thunder would not herald the rains, nor would the sun make the grain swing heavy in the fields. The crickets would not sing at harvest-time, nor the birds come together in clouds to fly south in late autumn. Nor would the earth fall into its cold sleep in winter and prepare to awake in the spring.

As long as the king did his duty and the seasonal cycle proceeded normally, his people supported him in his awesome post, removed from their sight behind the towering walls of his palace at the heart of the city. But if things went wrong, battles were lost or plague struck, then it was considered that the king had lost touch with heaven, and a new ruler must step into his place. Thus, the Chinese ruler was himself a servant of the universe, replaceable if he failed to keep the heavenly machinery going. As dynasties rose and fell, king replaced king without the basic patterns of Chinese society being changed, just as earthen walls were built upon earthen walls after floods or invasions, without altering the basic plan of the Chinese city.

Apparently the Shang people believed in an even higher power than their king. Christian missionaries of the nineteenth century were hopeful that the term "Ti" was a Chinese version of the western "God." But modern scholars are less sure exactly what "Ti" stood for, except that it was the name of a deity called "Sky."

Between the sky above and the earth underneath, the primitive Chinese and his king stood together, and all created things took their places on one or the other side of a great divide. As men of later dynasties explained it, "Yang" were the things upright and good, harmonious and filled with light—male individuals, and the sky itself. "Yin" were the things of darkness and confusion—female individuals and the damp earth running with rivers. If every man and woman, from emperor down to the farmer's wife, performed his duties in the right way, these opposite forces would rest in balance throughout creation—in the world at large, within the family, and in each person's life and body. But if the rituals were performed sloppily, Yin and Yang would fall out of balance and catastrophe occur. Of all the rituals at which the king presided, none was more urgently necessary for keeping Yin and Yang in balance than the spring plowing. "In the first month of spring," says a chronicle of this time, written in the Chou period, "the Son of Heaven shall wear green robes with pendants of green jade. His food shall be wheat and mutton, his dishes rough-surfaced and with wide mouths to represent coming-forth . . . Selecting a lucky day, with his charioteer and leading the chief ministers, his princes and officials, he shall personally plow the field of god." Setting a wooden plow into the furrow, the king made the first break in the earth's crust, opening it to the elements and calling forth from it grain and flowers and mulberry leaves and all the other growing things. "Then," continues the chronicle, "the vital force of Heaven (the Yang) comes down; the vital force of earth (the Yin) rises up, and the grass and trees begin to put forth leaves." Without any break, this ritual was carried out by Chinese emperors from the Shang Dynasty until the last spring of the Manchu Dynasty in our century.

And what were those mysterious "dragons' bones," whose appearance on Wang's table and in Farmer Li's field had led to the discovery of the Great City? They were communications written to Ti, asking how the day-to-day chores and duties ought to be carried out. "If the King goes to the field, will the harvest be good?" "If we perform the sacrifice, will grandfather recover from his illness?" "Will the enemy attack at dawn?"

A priest accepted the question from a petitioner. He wrote it in Shang characters with an awl on a flat bit of bone or the shell of a tortoise. Touching the bone with a red-hot poker, he cracked it into many fine lines. Then, probably relying on common sense and his own experience of how events usually proceeded, he would interpret the hidden language of the cracks. Often, the king's name was mentioned, together with puzzling phenomena like eclipses, which frightened the people and made them wonder if they had omitted some important part of their duties. It was from this combination of names and datable events that Shang history was finally pieced together, and the sequence of events proved to be just as the histories had described them.

During these same three decades of the twentieth century, scientists had followed other leads to extend the structure of historical fact back even before the Shang. One trail of unmarked "dragons' bones" led to a lode of petrified dinosaur bones from which bits had been chipped off over the centuries by villagers who lived nearby. Thus, it was shown that in prehistoric times, China was as rich in reptile life as western Europe and America, and that the north as far as the Gobi Desert was once a blooming region of well-watered marshes.

In 1926, Dr. J. Gunnar Andersson, a Swedish engineer who had spent many years exploring in China, reported the finding, in a clay-choked cave southwest of Peking, of two teeth apparently belonging to a prehistoric man. Later, Dr. Pei Wen-chung found the skull now called the "Peking Man," which is known to be a near contemporary of the European Neanderthal Man. Now the West could no longer call itself the sole birthplace of the human species, as nineteenth century European scholars liked to do, for the Asian family tree had roots just as deep in time.

Gunnar Andersson was also responsible for excavations which led to the sorting out of many New Stone Age peoples who preceded the Shang on the plains of North China. Several waves of these people had succeeded one another or lived separated by great distances. They lived in farming communities, probably in pits dug into the earth and roofed over with reeds, much as the unfortunates of the Great City Shang continued to do. The last of these peoples, named for the thin, black pottery they made, apparently overcame the others, at about the time kings were first rising to power in the Nile River valley in Egypt.

These Black Pottery people invented two clay vessels which have been made and used in China by every people and every dynasty that followed: one was a "hsien," or steamer pot for cooking rice and vegetables; the other

A

Bronze vessels, with fantastic mixtures of design and animal features, were used by ancient Chinese for their religious rites.

B

A "Li," or three-legged pot, first used in prehistoric times for cooking over fires; then, in bronze, for ritual sacrifices.

As early as the Shang and Chou Dynasties, magnificent works of art were made by Chinese craftsmen, then buried in the tombs of kings or used in holy rites. Lost in the earth for millenia, the bronzes were turned up from time to time by grave robbers, but the stone carvings (right) were only found for the first time when the Shang tombs were excavated in the 1930s. As bronze-workers, the early Chinese had no equals on earth: no one knows yet how they learned to cast molten metal into such complex shapes as these ferocious animal-headed vessels.

C

was a "li," or three-legged pot which could be set straddling a bonfire to cook the contents at an equal temperature on all sides. But if the "li" remained an unchanging form throughout Chinese history, the pictograph, or written character, for this object underwent a certain subtle transformation which suggests how the Chinese language itself evolved over centuries.

The character for this particular "li" is shaped like the cooking pot, an object so simple yet so functional that cast in permanent bronze, it was adaptable for use in religious rituals by both the Shang and the Chou people. These bronze "li" were used for making offerings to the ancestors and the gods, for preparing libations to be spilled upon the earth. Often they bore inscriptions that described which gods and ancestors were summoned to the ritual, and which earthly worshipper wished thereby to increase his standing with them. Thus, this "li" came to mean also, "ritual." Later still, as philosophers stretched the written language to express more subtle ideas, they suggested that "li" also implied a general rule of conduct, a correct way of performing a ritual and also of conducting oneself in life.

"Only when ornament and substance are blended together do you get the true gentleman," explained Confucius, describing exactly the New Stone Age people's favorite cooking pot—a perfect marriage of shape and function.

There is still a period of some thousand years in Chinese history that remains a mystery. From the height of the Black Pottery culture until that first, datable moment when the Shang warlord P'an Keng swept down on their thriving settlement, no one knows what happened. Who, really, were the Shang? When they appear, suddenly, on the scene of history, it is as if they sprang forth like the Greek goddess Athena, fully armed and ready to command the world. Already they have their heavenly power Ti and his envoy, the windy Dragon. Also, they know how to write, that marvelous invention that came to men of three lands at much the same time: Egypt, Mesopotamia, and China.

And, quite as important for their future, they knew how to cast bronze. For many centuries, the rare Shang bronze "li" and other vessels that grave robbers brought to light were prized above all other Chinese antiquities. After the digs at Anyang had been completed, it was clear that Shang superiority really depended on the hefty swords, shields, and bronze-hubbed chariots in which they had descended, like the Dragon itself, in a whirlwind of noise and dust, to build their new world on the plains of China.

Chapter III   In Search of The Way

Once upon a time, Chuang Chou dreamed that he was a butterfly,
a butterfly fluttering about, enjoying itself. It did not know that it
was Chuang Chou. Suddenly he awoke with a start and he was Chuang
Chou again. But he did not know whether he was Chuang Chou who
had dreamed that he was a butterfly, or whether he was a butterfly
dreaming that he was Chuang Chou. Between Chuang Chou and the
butterfly there must be some distinction. This is what is called
the transformation of things.

(SOURCES OF CHINESE TRADITION)

After a time, a rival group of Chinese people, led by a western warlord named Wu, challenged the Shang. Wu gathered his forces and marched toward the east, conquering various Shang settlements as he went, and finally storming the Great City itself and killing the last ruler there. Remnants of the Shang people fled farther east where, for a number of years, they went on performing the old rites of sacrifice to their ancestors as if that way they might at least maintain their power in the spirit world. But ultimately even this practice was stopped, and the Shang ghosts joined in oblivion those of other fallen kings and commoners.

But the Chou people, as the new masters were called, recognized that their predecessors had a richer civilization than their own. "Study the old, accomplished men of Shang," one Chou philosopher wrote, "that you may build your heart and know how to teach the people." Later dynasties, too, looked to the past, to both the Shang and Chou ancestors, as founders of the civilization of which they were, they felt, enjoying only a late flowering.

So the Chou took over Shang beliefs and rituals, adopted their written language and went on sending messages to Ti via the oracle bones. Also, they went on casting bronze vessels to use in their sacrifices, often now adding long passages of writing to tell how such a one was bestowed upon such and such a prince, for valor, or for special service to his king.

Western Chou power endured for some four centuries, until pressure from barbarian tribes in the north and rival warlords from within combined to bring it down. In 770 B.C., mounted hordes from the northwest galloped south and captured the Chou capital. Remnants of the Chou fled east, as the Shang had before them, and set up their own capital near the modern town of Lo-yang. There followed several centuries of social unrest, which bear the names, in Chinese chronicles, of Late Chou, or the Spring and Autumn period and the time of the Warring States.

During these years, rival cities sprang up here and there along the great waterways of north China. Wherever good land and nearby hills combined to make a site secure, a warlord might command his band of followers and the slaves he had taken in battle to raise up pounded earth walls for a settlement. There he would rule, in splendor and isolation, until a rival came to give the challenge. Thus, each lord ruled as he desired in his own domain, and fitful cruelty to men prevailed in some places, while others probably were ruled by men of wisdom and restraint.

During this time of challenge and individuality, some people began to ask themselves rather basic questions about the nature of man. Is he, they asked and as Chuang Chou dreamed, free as a butterfly to range the invisible airs? Or is he made of flesh and bone, subject to death and to the need to get along with other men in society? These were issues so basic that the answers worked out then have been taken ever since by the Chinese for the right ones.

Confucius was the most famous of these questioners. He was probably born in 551 B.C. When he grew up, he spent many years traveling from city to city, asking to be admitted, to teach and to question. Possibly he hoped always to find some wise king who would take his advice and create the perfect, harmonious state. But he was, apparently, unlucky in this respect. "Hidden orchid," he called himself, meaning that he felt his talents were wasted, flowering unnoticed by other men. But history did not permit the orchid to remain hidden, for after Confucius' death, his remembered "sayings" were put together with those of other men who agreed with him, to create the large body of writing called the Confucian Analects. Other so-called "Confucian Classics" included poetry and ethics, snatches of ancient historical documents, old speeches, and comments on the lives of kings of the Shang and early Chou dynasties, all worked into a tapestry on the general theme of Confucius' basic idea: "Fan Hsu asked about knowledge. The Master said, 'It is to know men.' Fan Hsu asked about benevolence. The Master said, 'It is to love men.'"

Confucius was not concerned with absolute truth, like Plato, who lived two centuries later in the West. Nor was he passionately interested, like Aristotle, in studying nature. Abstract, or "scientific" questions—how the universe sprang into being, how atoms and crystals and cells multiply themselves in all the forms of evolution, how reality coincides or conflicts with our inner vision just as shadows are reflected on the walls of a cave—questions which troubled philosophers of the West, Confucius ignored. For him, the urgent questions concerned men's lives in society, what kind of behavior they should adopt to make their lives useful and harmonious.

Loyalty seemed to Confucius the cornerstone of the successful life: loyalty within the family, and loyalty of each man to his superior. A son's life, for example, belonged wholly to his father and his family, to protect them and continually do them honor. A daughter's life belonged to her father, first, and then her husband. Death did not lessen these heavy burdens of responsibility. When a parent died, a man must leave his job in the city and go live in a rough hut close to the grave, wearing white mourning clothes, smearing his face with mud, sleeping on reeds and continually, for three years, making sacrifices to the spirit. Heavily the past weighed upon Confucius and the Confucian Chinese: the dead were the ones most honored. They had been better and more correct in their ways than the living. The years that had vanished behind the horizon were the best ones, and the Superior Man trained himself to be a living memorial to those gone.

Did Confucius really believe in this spirit world? It is hard to know, for the Classics were rewritten and added to over centuries until the small seed of Confucius' own words was overgrown with later additions. Perhaps he simply conceived of a society bound to its own roots as a more robust plant

Ink-rubbing, made in the eighteenth century from a design cut into stone, of the imagined features of the great Confucius, who lived some two thousand years earlier.

than one buffeted—as Western societies have been—by winds of change and revolution. The Confucian way, however, imposed an inner rigidity on Chinese society during the two thousand years which followed. Even in a period like the T'ang, when the country's energy was directed outward toward other civilizations, foreign trade and new ideas, still great stress was put on the Classics. In the examinations that ambitious Chinese youths then took to enter government service, Confucian studies were fundamental. There was, then and later, little room in China for the man of differing intellectual opinion, the eccentric, the experimenter. Men who felt moved by anti-social or radical ideas were more likely to choose painting or poetry as their field, for here, particularly in the T'ang and later periods, they could contrive to avoid social pressures to an extent and find peace in the countryside.

In the West, out of the ferment produced by men of radical ideas about political and social questions, many original forms of government and art evolved. The Confucian family, and its greater reflection in the emperor and his people, remained frozen in the old pattern until the twentieth century. Mao Tse-tung well knew that if he did not break this nucleus of resistance to social change, he would never succeed in setting Chinese youth free to build a communized society.

The other great teacher of the Late Chou period was Lao-tzu. This poetic philosopher may have lived in the sixth century B.C., or perhaps he never lived at all, but the ideas which are ascribed to him were much in the wind at that time. Lao-tzu, it was said, became disgusted with all human society and got onto his ox to ride off to the Western Paradise. However, at the Great Wall a soldier stopped him and requested a few words of wise advice about how to conduct his affairs. In response, Lao-tzu dictated his great work, a long, mystical series of prose-verses, the *Tao Te Ching,* and then rode off into the sunset.

The substance of Lao-tzu's teachings is that, behind all nature—behind the fertile earth, behind the man and his ox, and the river and the moon— is an invisible essence called "Tao." The best thing for men to do, he said, was to forget about society's problems and sorrows, to try to clear one's mind to feel in tune with "Tao." Confucius' ideas were later adopted as the state religion by many rulers of north China, but Lao-tzu's ideas took root particularly among the mountain and forest people of south China, lonely people whose huts were hidden in mist much of the time, who farmed or chopped firewood or meditated under soaking gray rains.

Taoist practitioners found various life-styles compatible with their various shades of belief. Some artists and philosophers remained Taoists in spirit, living close to nature. Other Taoists in later centuries threw themselves into the practice of magic. They believed that, if they could tap the invisible "Tao," they might be invested with great energy and power. They tried to discover ways of setting the spirit free, or curing diseases, or turning rocks into pure gold. Many a later emperor, at the same time that he performed the Confucian sacrifices to his ancestors, also urged his Taoist sorcerers to get on with their Elixirs of Immortality. Rooted in the ancient worship of Ti the sky, the dragons of wind and rain, and the earth, Taoism appealed particularly to a school of later Chinese artists who painted landscapes and wrote poems showing how the same rhythms embrace all nature and affect the meditative man as well. "I have three treasures," says the *Tao Te Ching*. "The first is called love; the second is called moderation; the third is called not venturing to go ahead of the world." What the Taoist way of thinking contributed to later Chinese society was an ability to endure periods of social stress and political chaos by retreating into an inner world. Thus in times of war or foreign occupation, some Chinese were always able to maintain their aloof balance and even a feeling of superiority to passing events.

The Confucian philosophers and Lao-tzu shared one idea: a confidence in man's nature and his ability to achieve a good destiny if he is fortunate enough to meet with good experiences in the course of his life. "The trees of the new mountain were once beautiful," wrote Mencius, Confucius' principal follower. But then, he explained, "they were hewn down with axes and bills—and could they retain their beauty?" Then, returning to man, he went on, "And so also of what properly belongs to man . . . hewn down day after day, can it—the mind—retain its beauty?" In this way, Mencius suggested that compassion and understanding are better tools for educating men than harsh punishments which might crush or deform their spirits.

However, some two hundred years after Confucius lived, a school of thinkers came forward who held dramatically different ideas about human nature and society. Man, they said, was basically of an evil predisposition. He must be whipped into shape, trained with brutal efficiency and ruled by drastic law. These men, in fact, placed all their reliance on something which

41

had seemed, to Confucius, of less matter than the good character of the ruler: law. In the West, many different peoples invented bodies of law that rode over the heads of kings and subjects alike, making them, ideally, all subject to the same punishments and rewards. But in China, the benevolent ruler, acting as a mediator between Ti and the people, was subject only to his own intuition of the right, and to patterns of action which he had learned from the past.

Chief among this group of law-conscious men, was Shang Yang. China's stability, as he saw it, depended on two things: her rich farmlands and her fearless war machinery. All other occupations—art, music, philosophy, the study of history—were only, to Shang Yang's mind, threats to the ordered movement of government.

Shang Yang was employed as an advisor to the ruler of the state of Ch'in, in the west of China. Now, under his counseling, the Ch'in forces began to move eastward, toppling one feudal city after another "as a silkworm devours a mulberry leaf," burning and destroying everything in their way. One idea alone inflamed the Ch'in ruler: he wanted to unify China into a single empire.

Once he had completed his conquest of all China, in 221 B.C., this ambitious warlord took a step to glorify himself above all the rulers of the past. Setting the title "Ti" next to his king-name, he called himself Shih Huang-ti, Son of Heaven, First Emperor. Thus, in one stroke, he lifted himself onto a historical pinnacle and established the principle that, by adopting the magical suffix "ti," the ruler might incorporate the very powers of Heaven. Henceforth, all Chinese rulers followed his example: we call them Emperors, the Sons of Heaven.

Two centuries later, the same idea occurred to another young ruler in the West. Crowning himself with a laurel wreath, the young Octavius of Rome, nephew of Julius Caesar, took the title "Augustus," or "Most High," to distinguish himself and his future reign from those of the republican Roman leaders who had preceded him.

As a matter of practical fact, both Huang-ti and the young Octavius were faced with the same problem. Each had to find a way rapidly and decisively to bind together a vast population, with different languages and customs, into a single body of loyal supporters. The symbol each man chose to represent his Empire, to fly upon his battle standard and to adorn his official documents—the clawed eagle of Rome, and the dragon—rode high over the heads of these people, giving them a focus for their thoughts about the new political structure to which they belonged.

Now, Shih Huang-ti set out to pull the parts of his empire together in actuality as well. He laid taxes on the peasants and with these monies built a formidable series of canals to link the natural waterways. Now he could move from north to south and westward in his enormous domains. Next, he swept thousands of peasants from their farmlands into his service to construct the Great Wall. Across 1500 miles of mountains and gorges, this fortification was drawn. To maintain it, and to support the armies that patrolled it, masses of farmers were moved up and set to work to cultivate the land in the northern marches.

In another decisive stroke, Shih Huang-ti reformed the written Chinese language, simplifying once and for all the hundreds of characters that had grown more complex since Shang times. Forever after, the Chinese written language would be a binding agent, for though many dialects may be spoken in the parts of the Central Kingdom, almost all these people can read the official writing.

These reforms had not been achieved without the exercise of cruel force. Soon, a number of scholars of the old Confucian ideas began to speak against Shih Huang-ti and to urge the people to turn back to principles of harmony and kindness. Now, a minister named Li Ssu spoke out, and the Emperor took his counsel. "Your servant suggests that all books in the imperial archives save the memoirs of Ch'in be burned. Those who dare to talk to each other about the Book of Odes and the Book of History should be executed . . . those who have not destroyed their books are to be branded and set to build the Great Wall."

A holocaust followed. After the flames had died down, only fragments of the great classic literature were left—some books on medicine, magic, agriculture and a few other non-political subjects. In the Han, T'ang and later dynasties, those fragments would be treasured over all later works, just as we in the West fill museums with the broken fragments of Greek and Roman statues which survived the sack of Rome and the collapse of the ancient Mediterranean world.

All the same, the political basis and the philosophical rationale on which dynasties to come would be organized had been set by the third century B.C. Much was lost forever, but generations in the future would strengthen the ties binding them to the old, accomplished men of Shang.

43

Chapter IV Beyond the North Wind

. . . the Arimaspi, a one-eyed people, and beyond them,
the gold-guarding griffins, and beyond them, the
Hyperboreans who reach to the sea."

(HERODOTUS)

*D*espite his attempts to put down rebellion, the "First Emperor" ultimately failed to consolidate his First Empire, perhaps simply because of the
harsh means he had taken to try to force it into being. At his death, he had
left little untested in his hunger to control both the land and the upper airs.
He had even enlisted a band of Taoist magicians to try to stave off his fatal
illness. They did their best, plying him with doses of Elixir of Immortality,
but notwithstanding, Shih Huang-ti joined his ancestors. After his death,
the Empire fell into revolt as local lords drew apart into their old feudal

strongholds. One of them eventually was capable of restoring peace and, in 202 B.C. founded the dynasty known as Han.

In that year, on the great plain bounded by the Yellow River, a capital city was laid out. "The Emperor planned here a base of imperial power that would last a hundred thousand years," wrote Pan Ku, a great Han historian. This was the city Ch'ang-an, which, under T'ang rule, would reach its height of grandeur eight hundred years later.

Only a jumble of ruins remained even then of this Han metropolis, but it can be imagined, mightier than the Great City Shang but still laid out along similar lines, a square protected by towering walls and guard posts at each corner. Within, the old Shang and Chou architectural forms were repeated, only more richly. On rammed earth platforms stood vast but light-hearted structures of carved and gilded wood. "The rafters of the throne room of the Son of Heaven are to be hewn, rubbed smooth and polished with a fine stone," ordered an architect.

The Han emperors were lovers of nature: in their imperial gardens, roses and peonies bloomed, and orange trees and lilies. Goldfish ponds caught the sunlight between winding paths where one might meet a tame deer. Bronze statues of giants held up their hands to catch the dew, which Taoists believed contained the magical essence in its purest form. One part of the garden was reserved for the mulberry bushes on which silkworms fed. Here, on festival days, the empress and her ladies tied the branches with colorful silk streamers. The emperor, for his part, continued the already ancient traditions, plowing the fields in spring and planting the first seed in the earth.

Many Hans tombs have been found and excavated, walled with hollow bricks like those Aurel Stein found along the wall of the same epoch in Chinese Turkestan. These bricks often were stamped with the name and date of a particular emperor and were decorated with tiny images of monsters and battling soldiers in full armor. Though Chinese sculptors did not often use stone, during this time in history—perhaps because of contact with stone-workers of the Near East—they did choose this material, and that they did so was fortunate for us. Many Han carvings have survived. From them, we can know how the people looked and behaved.

A particularly electric energy seems to sweep all the men and beasts on a Han relief carving or painting. Often, these elements are put together into scenes with the jovial humor of a modern comic strip. One of these, for instance, shows some men in bulky robes and pointed hats trying

Artists of the Han Dynasty left many traces from which we can imagine the kind of life they knew. This clay model of a typical house is decorated with a flamboyant figure of a dragon on the lower wall, and a pattern of diamonds under the outstretched roof, which in reality might have been bright tiles laid on wooden rafters.

to snare a bronze pot that has fallen into a river. However, behind their backs, a dragon has emerged from the pot and bitten through the rope. Over the courtiers tumble as if they were actors in a movie, while birds beat their wings overhead, and out on the water, boatmen vainly try to fish up the pot with their lines.

Other stone carvings of the Han period are more ponderous, stable figures in the full round, of thick-limbed bears, lions, soldiers and noblemen. These were set up as guardians along the paths which lead toward important graves. Their task was to oversee the "spirit road," down which the ghost of the dead man might return if sufficiently delicious sacrifices were set out before the tomb.

Still other Han artists were busy experimenting with new shapes and finishes for pottery. Though the glazes they managed to achieve look rather muddy compared to the jewel-like glazes of the future, they still have a delicate, earthy charm. One poetic Han invention was an incense burner called a "hill jar". Round and stocky, lifted on small legs, the "hill jar" is shaped like a rocky mountain lapped by gentle waves. It represents the Taoist paradise, a mystical island said by the poets to lie somewhere in the eastern seas.

Han artists created a style full of electric energy and swift motion, perhaps inspired by the sight of galloping horses and alert hunters, which these early Chinese were familiar with. Yet an element of poetry was present in Han art too: above is a small incense burner, coated with a glaze still somewhat primitive yet gracefully earth-colored. It represents the Isle of the Blessed somewhere in the Southern Seas, to which, according to Taoist philosophers, fortunate men went after death.

Buildings and walls of the Han Dynasty were constructed and faced with tiles stamped in vibrant designs: on this tile from a Han tomb (above), flying witches, running horsemen and winged dragons pursue one another. The clam shell at the left is one of a pair, both of which were painted in bright colors with scenes of hunters and their prey. At the top, is a chariot.

Scholarship flourished in the Han courts too. Literary experts were set to work piecing together the fragments of Confucian writings which had survived the centuries. Also, the Han emperors set up a system of civil service. According to its still quite primitive program, young men from various parts of China could be recommended to government service. Once settled in a niche in the central bureaucracy, the lucky and hard-working youth could move up the social ladder, bringing glory to his family and greater security for himself than he would have enjoyed otherwise.

Thus it was not long before a new ideal life-style seemed to present itself to the Chinese youth. No more—and never again—was the feudal warlord with his ambitions considered a model man. Too often, his aggressive drive to power had led to the shattering of the empire. Now, instead, Chinese youths were encouraged to conduct themselves with the modest, uncomplaining reliability of the bureaucrat at his desk.

In 141 B.C., one of the great figures in Chinese history, Emperor Wu, came to the Han throne. Emperor Wu first spent his time launching campaigns against the northern barbarians; then he marched down into the southern districts, through the rich Yangtze and West River valleys. Now, south and north China were again linked under a single hand.

Within Ch'ang-an's walls peace prevailed during much of the Han Dynasty. But beyond, the Emperor was not unaware of a threat. The enemy against whom the Han felt most anxious to protect themselves were the Hsuing-nu, ancestors of the terrible Huns, who were gathering in ominous numbers at the north of the Wall. So Wu decided to send an ambassador to the rear of the Hsuing-nu territory to make contact there with one of their long-time enemies. Wu's plan was to catch the Hsuing-nu as if between two pincers and destroy them.

The imperial ambassador, Chang Ch'ien, set out on his dangerous mission but was taken prisoner by the Hsuing-nu. For many years, he was forced to roam with them between their grazing grounds. At last, he escaped and continued westward, but when he found the tribe he was looking for, it had forgotten its old enmities. So when, in 126 B.C., Chang Ch'ien again presented himself before his Emperor, he had to say that his mission was a failure. But Chang had accomplished something far more important for the future of China. He had wandered in western Asia as far as Bactria. There he had seen Greek-style cities left in the wake of Alexander the Great's campaign two centuries before. When he returned to the Dragon Throne, Chang could therefore report that he had seen "cities, houses, and mansions as in China," and in some of these cities, "large bamboos and cloth of Shu,"—cloth imported, apparently, from western China itself without the knowledge of men in the capital city. Across the mountain trails into India, goods must have traveled by horseback and then, unknown even to their Chinese suppliers, on to Bactria. Now Wu was doubly encouraged to push back the enemy and to clear out the northern marches for trade and travel between China and India and beyond. Eventually, he cleared the territory for Chinese passage as far north as the flats of Lop Nor, where Aurel Stein found Han traces. Thereafter, Wu sent some ten missions a year as far west as they could penetrate, to trade in gold and silk.

It seems impossible that contact could have occurred between men of East and West across these deserts and mountains before the days of modern equipment, but contact there apparently was—rare it is true, but enough so that even during the Late Chou period, vague rumors had reached the West of a land that lay "beyond the north wind." If similar rumors reached China, their traces have been lost, but a scant few are preserved in western documents. Probably, there were many brave men who set out then to discover what lay "beyond," but hardly a one returned to tell what he had seen.

One of these, perhaps, was named Aristeas. He was a Greek who lived around the seventh century B.C. His own report has vanished, but a Greek historian of a later day, Herodotus, had heard about him. Aristeas, he explained, had been beckoned by Apollo towards the place where the sun-god appeared each dawn. Somewhere out there, he had met nomad tribes, and from some of these men whose camels watered at the ends of the earth Aristeas had heard about "the Arimaspi, a one-eyed people, and beyond them, the gold-guarding griffins, and beyond them, the Hyperboreans who reach to the sea." Those Hyperboreans, we imagine, were people living in the eastern part of China during the Chou period.

At that time in history, what led men on into unknown lands was probably gold. The richest gold deposits were held by a nomad people called the Scythians, whose horses ranged the western Asian deserts around the Caspian Sea. "The Arimaspi," explained Herodotus, "steal it from the griffins." As if to honor these mythical guardians of their gold-deposits, both Scythian and Greek goldsmiths often used their images, eagle-winged and lion-clawed, to decorate their battle gear and their golden drinking cups. The

Scythians remained a link between the Greeks and the farther East for some centuries. Then they were driven out of their territory by other tribes, and the faint notion of China's existence faded for a time.

Eventually Greece was absorbed by Alexander the Great, who led his armies of exploration and conquest to the very border of Asia. Next after him came the garrisons of the Roman Empire, neighbor in time of the Han Empire in China.

As Rome grew rich and populous in the first centuries of our era, silk—"seres," as the Romans called it—replaced gold as the product most coveted from beyond the seas. Roman women doted on this marvelous, floating, washable material, which fell like clouds along the body. And China—"Seres"—was the only source of silk in the ancient world. Only in the gardens and groves of the Central Kingdom did the silkworm goddess sleep in her cocoon, awakening to feed on the sacred mulberry leaves. Long before Han times, silk-making had become an established industry in China.

Now, from the borders of China, by camel caravan, along the very oasis stops where Aurel Stein was to pass, the precious bolts of silk were transported to Near Eastern cities like Tyre and Sidon. There, the standard-size lengths were often unwoven, usually dyed glorious hues of purple or sunset rose, and rewoven into stuff so sheer it floated like gauze. Then it was loaded onto ships bound for the market ports of Italy like Pozzuoli, for delivery to Pompeii and Rome, or for the farther colonies of Spain, Gaul and Britain.

But of direct contact between the silk-makers of Han China and the silk-buyers of Rome there was none, for a people called the Parthians controlled the Near East and, shrewdly, would not tell where the precious product really came from. So East and West yearned toward each other across a great gulf of ignorance. "Ta Ts'in," wrote a Chinese envoy sent overland to learn what he could, "lies west of the sea and is known as the Land West of the Sea . . . the walls of cities are built of stone . . . the people are tall and have an air much like ours . . . their king has long wished to send an embassy to China." Another Chinese envoy, Kan Ying, traveled as far as that sea, the Caspian, but there he halted in dismay. "This sea is very wide," he told his Emperor. "With good winds, one may cross it in three months. But if the winds are poor, the trip may take two years. Moreover, there is something about this sea which makes people so long for their home that they often die of it."

From the other side of the divide, the Roman historian Pliny wrote his version too: "Behind this country, the sea comes to an end," he said. "In the interior of that country is a very great city . . . but it is not easy to get to . . . and few and far between are those who come from it."

The Han Empire endured until the early years of the third century A.D., when various groups inside the court began to agitate for their own power. One party consisted of the palace guard itself. Another, the Yellow Turbans, was led by ambitious Taoists. As early in the dynasty as the reign of Emperor Wu, it had been recognized that transference of the Heavenly Mandate after his death would be difficult and perilous, for the line of inheritance in China was complicated by the presence of children belonging to various wives of the Emperor. Savage competition often went on between members of the Emperor's own family. It was a pattern of violence often repeated in future years.

In 220 A.D., the Empire fell into three segments, each of which claimed to hold the true Mandate. These lasted only briefly. Meanwhile, new barbarian peoples were massing at the north, as they did whenever the imperial grip on that territory weakened. These desert nomads were ripe for conversion to a new religion, Buddhism, which had already begun to filter into China.

In the West, too, reverberations were beginning to be felt in the far reaches of the Roman Empire which in another hundred years would lead to its disintegration. Soon, to the unsophisticated and poor of the eastern Mediterranean world would come prophets of the new Christian religion which, like Buddhism in India, would offer something unique to its converts: a future of bliss for anyone, unfortunate though he might be in this life, who would open his heart to the word of a simple man of the people.

Chapter V   Barbarians and Pilgrims

And what are the thirty-two marks of the superman, turner
of the wheel . . . Buddha supreme?

1. He hath feet with level tread.

2. On the soles of his feet, wheels appear thousand-spoked . . .

11. His complexion is like bronze, the color of gold . . .

22. His jaws are as a lion's . . .

27. His tongue is long . . .

29. His eyes are intensely blue . . .

31. Between the eyebrows appears a hairy mole white and like
soft cotton down . . .

32. His head is like a royal turban . . .

(BIBLE OF THE WORLD)

During the reign of a Late Han emperor, Ming-ti, art and religious ideas from the far ends of the empire had been welcomed at court. At the Cloud Terrace of his palace in Lo-yang, "the art of the realm was assembled like clouds." Every one of these works of art was lost when the city finally was destroyed in 195 A.D., but the ideas sown there survived, and among these, one of the most portentous for Asia was the worship of Buddha.

The bare facts of Buddha's life have been overgrown with miraculous stories, just as have the events of Jesus' life. But certainly there was an individual born in the fifth century B.C. in the northeast of India who became, like Jesus, a great teacher and leader of men and whose myth would long outlast his lifetime. Like Jesus, Buddha gave voice to a doctrine rarely heard in the ancient world: compassion for all living things. Also like Jesus, Buddha promised that there would be an end to suffering for all men who followed his teachings in this life. These two radical new ideas in a world where hitherto only the sword had counted—a loving view of other people, and the eventual relief of pain—were what the enslaved and homeless, the poor and hungry, as well as the rich and powerful, yearned for.

In the land of Israel, the Evangelists took the simple facts of Jesus' birth in a stable and turned them into a subject fit for great artists; so too, throughout India, beautiful stories were soon told about Buddha's life. A white elephant, it was said, had come in a dream to the future mother of the god; three times it circled her bed, then lightly tapped her with his trunk. Later, her infant son sprang from her side as she stood resting under a tree. In a golden net, four goddesses caught the shining baby. Four kings, the guardians of East, West, South and North, held him upon a silver pillow for everyone to admire. Springing down, the infant began to walk; where he put his foot, lotus flowers bloomed.

Buddha was brought up in the gardens of his family's mansion, far removed from the sorrows and hardships of the surrounding city. After he grew to manhood and married, however, he three times eluded his guardians and rode out beyond his father's walls. There, each time, he encountered one of the very things his father had wished to protect him from: a man withered by old age, a man wracked by sickness, and the corpse of a dead man lying, according to the Indian custom, on a pile of wood ready to be burned. Siddhartha, as he was called, was horrified by these signs that life for many men was not tranquil and comfortable. On one further excursion into the city, he met a holy monk, one of the believers in the Hindu religion whose habit it was to wander from place to place, begging for alms and meditating upon the condition of life. Struck by the suggestion which he felt had been made to him from some divine source, Siddhartha abandoned his wife and child and set out to explore his world. It was his ultimate goal to make up his mind how men ought best to cope with their existence.

He spent some time with a band of Hindu monks. According to their beliefs, life was an on-rushing flood of events and things with no more reality than the images of a dream. Men, women, and all living things were born and reborn into this stream of "Maya" in various shapes throughout eternity. The shape they were reborn into depended on the amount of good or evil they had accumulated in lives gone by.

Siddhartha, however, felt that the Hindu explanation was only a partial one. Life as he observed it in the poverty-ridden, crowded cities of India indeed seemed to be simply a torrent of meaningless vitality. But Siddhartha felt there must be some way out of this round of unhappy rebirths, at least for the pious man who wished for such release. Thus he traveled on, wondering, until he felt overcome by fatigue and lay down to rest under a certain tree in the town of Gaya. There he fell into a dream, from which he awoke suddenly with the vision he sought: to be alive was to suffer pain and uncertainty—that much seemed true—but if a man conducted himself according to an "Eightfold Path" of action and thought, then he could escape the net and find peace in a state of nothingness, called "Nirvana." Instead of a future of infinite lives burdened from the infinite past with wrongdoings, one could hope for a forgiveness so total that no shred of guilt would remain to disturb the final sleep.

This teaching was received with joy by the people. Since the instant of his Enlightenment under the Bo tree, the youth Siddhartha had become "Buddha," the one who saves. People exchanged anecdotes about his life and his eventual death, but there were no pictures or statues to remind them of how he had looked, for he was not considered a god to be worshipped. His followers simply tried to abide by his instructions for the good life, practicing charity and gentleness, and meditating a great deal, trying to cast off the normal hungers which attach men to the things of this world.

Then, coinciding with the early years of the Han Dynasty, a certain king came to the throne of India who suffered greatly because of the bloodshed by which he had obtained his power. King Asoka wished somehow to atone for these terrible crimes and to free himself from the necessity of working them off in future incarnations. So he adopted the Buddhist teachings and passionately set about spreading Buddha's word throughout his kingdom and even beyond. Some scholars think Asoka's missionaries went as far west as Israel and there influenced the future forms of the religion which became Christianity.

At home, Asoka set up a series of columns throughout the land, at each important point of Buddha's wanderings and Enlightenment. Upon each column was a stone animal which might remind his people of one quality of the Buddha: a lion, for example, to symbolize his strength, or an ox, to symbolize his gentleness. The ruins of Asokan columns have been found in Bodgaya, Benares where Buddha preached his first sermon, and elsewhere. They were the first step Indian artists took in inventing an image of the Buddha which men might carry in their minds into the privacy of their homes, however poor those homes might be.

Slowly, Asoka's message began to spread westward and eastward. During the reign of Emperor Ming-ti, these teachings reached the Chinese court. Laboriously, Buddhist missionaries had inched their way through northwest India, then east along the Tun-huang road. The teachings they brought seem to have answered a hunger on the part of many Chinese for something neither Taoist poetry nor Confucian common sense gave them, for bit by bit Buddhism took root, and by 500 A.D., all the Central Kingdom knew the religion. The T'ang Dynasty was its period of greatest hold in the Central Kingdom.

By Ming-ti's time, the simple teachings of Buddha had been richly elaborated. Now he was actually worshipped as a god, who had come down to earth to rescue men from their sufferings, and an artistic form sufficiently suggestive had been invented so that men in different parts of Asia could unite in bowing before the same holy image. In the northwest of India, in a region called Gandhara, Indian sculptors working side by side with artists trained in styles of the late Roman Empire had put together an image for this man on the way to becoming a god. These early Buddhas were shown standing or seated with folded legs, garbed in Roman-style robes, with eager eyes and a youthful expression. More particularly, his body bore special signs which had been described in the holy sutras, or Buddhist scriptures. His ears were very long; on his brow was a third "eye" of wisdom; his hair curled in a thousand snailshells, and so on. Little sculptures of Buddha were carried along the silk trails, tucked into the pockets of the missionaries' robes; and where these pious pilgrims stopped for rest, they might paint a picture of the one who watched over their journey on the wall of a cave.

Probably it was because the coming of Buddhism coincided with the collapse of the Han Dynasty and the beginning of an era of turbulent foreign influence in China that it so effortlessly persuaded China to its ideals. As the fourth century drew on, barbarian tribes began to fling themselves against the Great Wall, and in 316, Tartar hordes from Mongolia broke through as far south as Ch'ang-an itself. Fanning out across the northern plains, the Tartars claimed all the old Han settlements in north China for their own. One watching from on high might have said that the whole civilized world, at this moment, was crumbling together, for the great city of Rome too was being overrun by barbarian hordes. Soon the western Mediterranean world would shrivel into the sleep of the Dark Ages.

In China, however, the outlanders realized at once that their culture could not compare to that of their victims, in spite of superior battle tactics and their heavily muscled "supernatural horses." So they adopted the Chinese language and settled down into Chinese cities, taking on Chinese ways. A later historian contemptuously noted that "barbarians are converted to the ways of the Central Kingdom as wind humbles the grass."

The most powerful of the non-Chinese peoples in north China during these years were the Wei. One of their leaders moved his capital down from the steppes to historic Lo-yang. Then he made a deliberate effort to bind his own people together with the Chinese by giving them all an official religion. The one he chose had, like himself, been born beyond the Great Wall.

"We were born out of the marches," a Wei official explained, "and though we are unworthy, we have obeyed our destiny and rule the Chinese as their prince. Since Buddha is a barbarian god, he is the very one we should worship . . ."

Having destroyed so much, now the Wei monarchs set out to rebuild the empire. Enthusiastically they raised up Buddhist temples and monasteries until Lo-yang alone had over a thousand. Some of these were only little shrines containing a relic or a holy statue. Others, outside the big cities, were enormous complexes of caves hollowed into cliffs, and contained numerous chambers filled with sculpture and painting, tended by resident monks. Soon a long chain of these cliff-shrines led from Gandhara all the way into China. The earliest of them is in Bamiyan, in north India, where a figure of the Buddha over a hundred feet tall gazes out over paths and mountains as if the god were living within the very earth over which men plied their way. Other, later cave complexes have been found at Yunkang in north China, at Lungmen near Lo-yang and elsewhere; those Aurel

Stein discovered at Tun-huang were only one step in this sacred pilgrimage route.

In the forms of the sculpture themselves, too, are fascinating evidences of how Buddhist ideas gradually swept the eastern world. The first carvers in the new faith were from India or Turkestan; in caves of this time there is not a single evidence of Chinese hands, neither inscriptions in Chinese language nor images in the energetic style of the old Han artists. Then, a great school of artists arose working in the employ of the Wei monarchs, speaking and writing their crude Chinese, carving figures of Buddhas which hold their knees in stiff, tense angles, their wrists flexed, as if in memory they still clutched the reins of horses. Later still, as pure Chinese artists, trained in the sophisticated workshops of the T'ang emperors, became disciples of Buddha, the figures they made were sensuously modeled, with dreamy, fish-like features, wearing the fluttery scarves and jewels of court costumes.

As time went on, Buddhism grew heavy with conflicting ideas and began to split into sects. Now it was believed that many different Buddhas had appeared in and vanished from the universe during different cosmic epochs. In the caves of Lungmen, a melancholy inscription described the confusion which many felt when confronted by the teachings of scholarly monks out of touch with the people: "One Buddha came into the world too long ago in the past for us to be able to reach him. Another Buddha will come to earth too far in the distant future for us ever to catch up with him . . . when we think of ourselves, lost in between, we are filled with grief . . ."

Medieval Christians, over-awed by the idea of the Trinity, invented a host of saints to mediate between themselves and the mystical Godhead. So, during this period, Buddhist believers invented a number of tender beings who moved, as it were, in a half-world between the earth and Nirvana, mercifully showering rewards on the good and receiving sinners in compassionate forgiveness. One of these was Kuan-yin, goddess of mercy, who felt pity for each human being suffering in the coils of life. Kuan-yin was shown by artists dressed in soft scarves, adorned with necklaces, lifting her hand tenderly and smiling upon whomever needed her ministrations. Another was the Maitreya Buddha, a saint who, it was believed, would appear in future generations to save the lost and homeless of the future. Another was Amitabha Buddha, Lord of the Western Paradise, where music and flowers filled the air and the blessed might live in happiness forever. This was a more appealing goal than Nirvana, to which the Buddha had austerely directed his followers. Anyone who kept the name Amida upon his lips was promised an eternity of bliss there among hills which lay blue in mist.

About 516, a teacher named Bodhidarma came to the eastern city of Lo-yang from somewhere in the west, perhaps from Persia. His message was that no amount of prayer or study of the scriptures would help prompt that sudden flash of Enlightenment which the Buddha had experienced under the Bo tree. Instead, said Bodhidarma, one should work to clear one's mind of all extraneous thoughts and to give up every vestige of striving for worldly success or knowledge. And then, when the spirit was ready, any sudden and surprising shock, like a clout on the head, or a loud noise, might jolt one over the border into that mystical condition of Knowledge. Ch'an Buddhism, or Zen as it was later called in Japan, came as a refreshing relief to many Buddhists who, in spite of their desire for a more refined condition of life, could not afford to lay down their responsibilities and become scholarly monks. What Bodhidarma preached was really a return to the old, personal, spiritual search which the Buddha had urged. But the mass of people are rarely content with simple explanations for long, and soon a host of fanciful tales were being told about Bodhidarma too, and how he sailed off across the Yangtze River on a reed to preach his doctrine to the South.

As Buddhism became more complicated and teachers vied with one another to attract converts, some Chinese students of the religion made up their minds to travel to India to find out exactly what the Teacher had said. In 602, sixteen years before the beginning of the T'ang Dynasty, the most famous Buddhist pilgrim of all was born—Hsüan-tsang, "patron saint" of Aurel Stein. Hsüan studied at the famous Pure Land Monastery in Lo-yang when he was a youth and there became befuddled by monkish lectures on subjects like "Eighteen Kinds of Nothingness." So he decided to make the pilgrimage to India and find the true doctrine.

First he toughened his body for the long overland trek. He learned several exotic languages—Sanskrit, the Buddha's own tongue, and those of the tribesmen he would meet on the way. Then he set off.

He journeyed northward, not stopping at Tun-huang which still lay in ruins after centuries-long occupation by barbarians. But he did visit the oasis city of Turfan. The local king invited him to settle down and teach there, but Hsüan regretfully pushed on westward, across the ice-covered mountains, to the rich merchant city of Samarkand and even to Balkh, where Alexander the Great had tried to bind East and West together by taking a Bactrian bride. Finally, in deep snow, Hsüan crossed back over the Hindu Kush mountains, down to Bamiyan.

The great rock carvings and cave temples lay nearby. One day, Hsüan decided to visit a particularly famous cave where it was said the Buddha's shadow still could be seen. He was climbing toward the cave when five robbers jumped out from behind a tree. But Hsüan bowed with courtly courage and announced, "Even robbers are men. As I am on my way to worship the Buddha, I am not afraid, even if I were to meet a pack of wild animals, much less gentlemen like you!" Humiliated, the robbers went away.

Later, Hsüan made his way to the border of Nepal, to the very tree under which Buddha had sat. Nearby, at a place called Nalanda, was a great monastery founded several hundred years earlier, still the most important Buddhist center in the world. Ten thousand monks lived and worked at Nalanda, using a great library of scrolls on philosophy, mathematics, medicine and Buddhist scriptures—all the rich learning of India's past. From one hundred nearby villages, tithes were collected of rice, oil, cheese, milk and betelnuts so that the monks were free of all practical worries. Hsüan described the scene with awe, for it almost certainly overshadowed any structures he had so far seen at home. "A red wall surrounds the whole abbey," he wrote. "Its towers are arranged in correct order of height; pavilions adorned with coral lift into the air like the tops of trees; soaring domes stand in the middle of clouds and their pinnacles seem to float above the vapours of the sky."

Indian scientists were at that time far in advance of the rest of the world: "Observatories are lost in the mists of the morning," wrote Hsüan. "Their upper rooms tower above the clouds. From the windows one may see how winds and clouds ever produce new shapes of beauty, and above the soaring roofs, the conjunctions of the sun and moon may be seen.

"All around, the deep translucent ponds bear on their surface the blue lotus with its spread petals, intermingled with the Kanaka flower of deep red . . .

"The outside courts, in which are the priests' chambers, are four stories high. The stories have dragon-carvings, and colored eaves, and the pearl-red pillars, carved and ornamented, the richly adorned balustrades and the roofs covered with tiles all reflect the light in a thousand shades . . ." At the end of the tenth century, Nalanda and all its libraries burned to the ground, but not before missionaries and traveling artists had sown its ideas throughout southeast Asia and as far eastward as Japan.

Hsüan, for his part, turned back to China. People everywhere he went begged him to stay in India. They argued that China was a land of barbarians, where neither man nor the law was respected. But Hsüan explained that China was now ruled by a wise emperor and populated by men of good heart. Charity was practiced in every Chinese city, he said; temples there contained clinics and dispensaries. No Chinese peasant, however rude his life, however far he lived from the capital city, was allowed to suffer without the Emperor's concern. Moreover, he went on to say, both China and India were part of the "Great Island of the Rose Apple Tree," and it was his duty to return to his side of the Island to preach the Truth.

So Hsüan recrossed the terrible mountains, near White Stone Peak, where winds blow so fiercely no bird can lift its wings. Along the way, he made note of strange tribes—the White Huns, whose women wore horned headdresses, and a people mysterious for their amber hair and eyes the color of lapis. He returned through Khotan, famous for its gem bazaars, where one could find jade the color of "crystallized moonlight"—"City of Five Forts, dear to the earth goddess, whose mines are rich in jade." By this time, the young T'ang regime was firmly installed and had cleared out the oasis towns—Turfan, Kucha, Khotan—and reopened the route to India for easy passage. The Emperor of China now, and second ruler of the T'ang Dynasty, was T'ai Tsung. Though he himself claimed to be descended from the Taoist sage Lao-tzu, in his eagerness to consolidate his new power, he set out to court the Buddhists. One day, he paid a visit to a Buddhist temple. Apologetically, he said, "Lao-tzu is my ancestor. One has to honor one's ancestors because they are the very roots of one's life. I am afraid you are very cross about that." Then he gave the monastery a large sum of money to enlarge its living quarters and gardens.

When he heard that the famous traveling monk, Hsüan-tsang, was on his way home from the land of the True Doctrine, T'ai Tsung sent an official party to escort him safely into Ch'ang-an. They led him through the Gate of Brilliant Virtue, along the broad central avenue lined with graceful shade trees, and then turned left into the western marketplace, where the camels of overland caravans swayed to their knees to discharge their goods and passengers. When Hsüan's crates and chests were unloaded, a train of monks led a procession to the Hung-fu monastery at the northwest corner of the city. All along the road, people gathered to throw flowers at Hsüan. But no one was allowed to touch his porters, lest they jostle the precious boxes of souvenirs he had brought from India. One hundred and fifty pellets of the flesh of Buddha himself, a golden statue of Buddha, one of silver, and many of sandalwood were in the baggage. So were over six hundred books and scrolls, containing the authoritative words which Hsüan had traveled so far to obtain.

For the rest of his days, Hsüan labored at translating these and writing his own Record of Western Countries. A room was provided for him in the Meditation Cloister of the Hung-fu monastery. There the Emperor himself often came to watch him work and to ask questions. "Looking at these Buddhist works," T'ai Tsung said, "is like gazing at the sea or sky. So lofty one cannot measure the height, so profound one cannot plumb the depths." Indeed some of the Buddhist writings may have seemed clouded with abstruse ideas to a Chinese mind, trained in the straightforward precepts of Confucius. "There comes a time," runs one teaching on the *Becoming of the World,* "when, sooner or later, after the lapse of a long, long time, this world passes away. And when this happens, beings have mostly been reborn in the World of Radiance . . . There also comes a time when, sooner or later, this world begins to re-volve. When this happens, beings who have deceased from the World of Radiance usually come to life as humans. And they become made of mind, feeding on rapture, self-luminous, traversing the air . . ." "Confucius, Tao and our other schools, compared with it," said Emperor T'ai Tsung, "are like mere puddles measured against a mighty ocean."

Even after the Emperor died, in 649, Hsüan labored on. He worked by lamplight through the late evening. At dawn he arose to give lectures, to watch over his assistants, to visit his factory which was producing figurines of the Buddha.

Finally Hsüan grew old, but even still, the new Emperor kept him at his labors. Now the old man pleaded to be allowed to leave the pressure of the city. "Let me escape the noise and dirt," he begged. "Let the elk and deer be my companions. Let me follow the mallard and the crane. Some slab of rock shall be my bed, some simple tree my roof . . ." But the

Emperor would not let him go. "You are the Bridge to Salvation," he said.

Not until he became feeble was old Hsüan-tsang permitted to retire. Before he left Ch'ang-an, he paid a farewell visit to a series of statues he had set up in a garden in the city. "Let us go to the orchid and mushroom valleys, so I can say good-bye to my Buddhas," he said. Probably, he also made a last trip to the Wild Goose Pagoda, a towering shrine which had been built to house his precious Indian texts. The Wild Goose Pagoda, with its upturned roofs like lifted wings, outlasted Hsüan and the T'ang emperors and stood on, miraculously unhurt, through the cataclysms of future dynasties. One of the only two T'ang monuments left, it still stands in the modern city of Sian.

Hsüan-tsang retired to the rambling, rustic Jade Flower Monastery in an old summer palace eighty miles outside Ch'ang-an. After he died, the hardships he had undergone in his youth were embroidered much as the life of Buddha himself had been. Chinese parents told tales of the zesty monk to their children, as western parents have recounted the adventures of King Arthur or Ulysses, using these heroes to teach certain lessons of life. But Hsüan's adventures probably would not have been remembered through history had his life not coincided with the coming to power of the T'ang emperors, who opened a three hundred-year epoch of equally exhilarating adventures, centered around the Palace of Great Brightness in the city of Ch'ang-an.

Chapter VI Reforging the Empire

During the years following the fall of the Han Empire, Buddhism, which slowly filtered throughout China, became a bond between Chinese of different customs and dialects, classes and political loyalties. But from every other point of view, this was a time of upheaval and dissension. The Wei were only one, though the most powerful and intelligent, of the several barbarian and Chinese groups who controlled various segments of what had once been a unified empire, and none of these succeeded in putting the broken pieces back together. Many of the old Confucian families that once held high positions in the North had fled to safety in the South where, in the swampy Yangtze River country, the horses of their barbarian pursuers were of no use. Memories of the great days of the Han court weighed heavily on these exiles, and they must have felt with bitterness and sorrow the loss of their empire after four hundred years of solidarity. A contemporary historian told how a party of exiled officials went one day for a picnic into the southern hills. There, they "drank and feasted. Chou Hou sat down among them and said, 'The scenery in general is no different here. It is just that there are other mountains and rivers.' Then, they all looked at one another and wept." They were, they felt, cut off from their roots, behind the "Great Difference Mountains."

Thus it was probably with an invigorating sense of renewal that, gradually during the middle years of the sixth century, a native Chinese people gathered the reins of power in the north once more. By 581, they once again controlled all of the Yellow River land, that historic region which had seen the rise and fall of several empires. That year, one individual proclaimed himself Emperor of the new Sui kingdom.

This first emperor of the Sui Dynasty, Wen-ti, commanded his architects to lay out a new city, to be the focus of Sui power and a worthy emblem of his new position. He proceeded as the ancient rules and superstitions dictated. First, his magicians used spells to determine just where the city should be laid out and on what day the work should commence. They chose a site near the banks of the Wei River, where it flows eastward into the Yellow River—the same place, in fact, where the old Han emperors had built their capital city. But Wen-ti's magicians warned him against building new walls upon the old ruins. Ghosts of men murdered in ancient battles inhabited that particular land, they said. Also, more practically, the ancient Han water supply had been fouled. So they drew their great square city outline nearby, but still within the protective arms of mountain ranges to the north and south. As it turned out, a number of Han ruins lay within the royal parkland and provided a sentimental outing place for later T'ang emperors who wished to meditate on the swift passage of time.

Hastily, so that Wen-ti would not have to delay his inauguration, lines of thousands of laboring coolies raised up eighteen-foot-high walls of pounded earth, as much as thirty feet thick in places. In the center of the south wall, they cut the main gate. Then, always following the ancient prescriptions for royal capital cities, they marked off rectilinear areas for a palace in the center of the city. Here the Son of Heaven would live and exert his magical power to communicate with Ti, the sky, focus of the universe itself. Next, the architects marked off an official marketplace. To the southeast of the palace city would lie the temple of the Emperor's ancestors; to the southwest, the altar dedicated to the ancient earth gods. Finally, a geometric grid of residential streets was plotted. In 583, Emperor Wen-ti rode ceremoniously into the half-finished city, which was destined to become, before long, one of the two greatest metropolises on earth, equalled only by Constantinople.

By 589, Emperor Wen-ti had extended his rule over south China as well as the North, proceeding with little opposition from exiles who rejoiced to welcome a native Chinese ruler to the throne again. Wen-ti and his son and heir, Yang-ti, held the imperial power for only thirty-six years. During that time, they set the foundations for the T'ang Dynasty, which rose upon their heels. Later Chinese historians, always anxious to praise the dynasty that had come out on top, painted the last of the two Sui emperors as an unworthy and evil man, whose excesses undermined the nation. Perhaps indeed he went beyond the bounds of what was necessary to pull a chaotic China back together, but probably, too, strong measures were needed, and what the Sui built endured for centuries.

Wen-ti recognized that one of the weaknesses of his enormous empire was the vulnerability of each province to disasters like drought or flood, which could lead to famine in one place while others grew fat. So he set up a number of state granaries near his new city, to keep it supplied even in times of local catastrophe. His son, Yang-ti, went further and built a new series of canals, which eventually joined the ancient waterways and natural rivers and struck out in new directions to link North and South, from Hangchow to Peking and west to Ch'ang-an. Though it might take as long as a year for a barge loaded with rice from the south or millet from the north to make the journey from end to end, still the extremities of the empire could be supplied and the emperor could travel about with splendor and comfort.

As an added precaution, Yang erected a new eastern capital on the site of ancient Lo-yang, and populated it with farmers and merchants from other parts of the country. To Lo-yang, which was nearer the great north-south waterway, the imperial court would occasionally move in future years when war or famine struck Ch'ang-an.

These and his other building projects were bitterly attacked by later historians writing about Yang's regime, for the suffering they caused the people. He ordered timber brought from the south to build palaces and temples in his new cities, and it was said of the workers that "four or five out of ten fell and died . . . every moon, carts were in view of each other on the road, carrying the dead bodies east and north." When the dragon boat of the Emperor sailed out upon the canal, towed by green ropes between banks green with willows, the villagers had to supply his enormous party with food. "The people caught with nets and snares until the water and land birds and beasts were almost exterminated," wrote a historian. "Bone, ivory, hides, hair and feathers were exacted . . . What was ordered in the morning had to be provided by evening."

At home, it was said that Yang had slaughtered the birds in his garden for down to stuff his pillows. On bitter winter days, he sent his shivering slaves to make the trees bloom with silken leaves. Slowly, as the trade routes overland to India were being reclaimed from the barbarians and as caravans of rich tribute began to arrive in the official marketplace of Ch'ang-an, Yang-ti's appetite for luxuries grew. Lion skins and costumed dancing girls, drinking goblets made of thin colored stone were brought to him, amber and lapis lazuli, pearls and bronze weapons, and always, new Buddhist sculptures and holy writings.

However, to force open and then maintain the passes and oases along the north route to the outer world, on which the flow of these goods depended, Yang-ti's forces were obliged to pit themselves against a new enemy, the Turks, who were slowly consolidating their numbers and taking on new strength. One day, in the year 615, Emperor Yang was out inspecting his frontier guard when he ventured to ride beyond the wall into open territory. Suddenly, a thousand Turkish horsemen swept down on the imperial party. The wife of the Turkish leader was a woman of Chinese origin. She managed to send a warning to her countrymen and Yang had just time to hide himself in one of the garrison posts that lined the Wall. But there he was trapped without provisions or a way to escape.

A young soldier, part Chinese, part Tartar, named Li Shih-min, was then stationed just behind the Chinese lines. He had already spent some years of apprenticeship in the rugged military world of the northwest frontier, and, though he was only fifteen, he knew the psychology of the enemy. His suggestion was to station groups of Chinese soldiers all along the Wall, and after night had fallen, to set off bonfires and make a great noise with drums and horns. The plan worked. The Turks were tricked into thinking a great rescue army was on the way. The Emperor was able to slip out of his hiding place and return to Ch'ang-an. But his reputation as a wise leader of men had been destroyed. Next, he irresponsibly ordered a large Chinese force into war with her eastward-lying neighbor, Korea, and his men were decimated when unexpectedly heavy snowfalls of winter bogged them down.

Soon the peasants, on whom the good health of the empire basically depended, became demoralized. Weighted down under the taxes which paid for these military expeditions, and frightened by rumors that they too would soon be conscripted into the army or into labor parties, many peasants abandoned their fields and slipped away into the hills where they could evade the imperial dragnets. There, they joined into bands and began to prey on travelers on the lonely highways below. "Bandits arose like bees," say the historical chronicles.

Finally, as if nature herself were joining the ranks to rid China of an unworthy emperor, famine struck the land. "At first, everyone peeled the bark off trees. Gradually, they ate the leaves. When the bark and leaves were all gone, they boiled earth . . . After this, men ate each other."

Hounded by his failures, Yang-ti finally gave up and sailed away down the Grand Canal for a haven in his beloved South. There he hoped to avoid the ominous destiny preparing itself at home.

A rumor had been circulating for some time in Ch'ang-an—perhaps fomented by a Taoist monk or magician—that the empire would only be saved by someone in whose family name was the character for "Li." Yang-ti had tried to exterminate all the males in Ch'ang-an who bore this name, but it was an impossible task. Meanwhile, in the northwest, Li Shih-min was gradually sharpening his powers, working surreptitiously, extending his influence over larger numbers of soldiers. His father, Li Yuan, was an important Sui military official, and probably helped set the stage for revolt, but, according to one historical view, it was Li Shih-min who, when he saw that conditions in the empire had reached the point of intolerable confusion, gathered a force of supporters and marched on Ch'ang-an. Before setting out, he enlisted the help of the eastern Turks. To win them over, he agreed that "population and land" would go to the Chinese forces, while "money and silk, gold and jewels would go to the Turks." More greedy than politically ambitious, "the Khan was greatly pleased."

The history of the T'ang Dynasty is still being written. Much of the detail of Li Shih-min's life and character is still disputed by modern scholars, who are also divided on the question of how much he actually did to install the Dynasty. But traditional chronicles describe the events somewhat as follows.

Li Shih-min marched south, taking the great state granaries set up by the Sui rulers as he went and distributing the grain to the suffering peasants. In gratitude, they threw their weight behind the young general until, according to the histories, some 90,000 troops were marching behind him. It was his plan to set his father, who had the title Duke of T'ang, on the throne. At first, the Duke had refused. Then he had been won over by the plan and agreed not to report his son to the imperial guard. "I love you," he reasoned. "How could I bear to report you?" Meanwhile, Li's sister, who was also a military and ambitious character, had gathered a "Heroines' Army" and was marching to meet her brother.

Through Squirrel Pass north of Ch'ang-an came the conqueror and took the city, while far away in his luxurious southern palace on the Yangtze, Emperor Yang-ti whiled away his time writing poetry and painting pictures. His courtiers tried to explain that Ch'ang-an was in a state of siege and then that Ch'ang-an had fallen to the rebels, but Yang could not bring himself to admit that his reign had ended. "Such a beautiful head!" he remarked one morning, combing his hair before a polished bronze mirror. "Who would dare cut it off?" The answer was nearby. A band of his own guards burst into the imperial chamber one morning and killed his beloved son. Yang begged them to let him end his own life with poison, but they strangled him with his silken scarf as he sat upon the throne. Then, with Yang's Empress and her train of women, the rebels set off for Ch'ang-an to welcome the new regime. In 618, Sui rule came to an end, and Li Yuan, the Duke of T'ang, ascended the Dragon Throne.

On an early summer day in the imperial palace in Ch'ang-an, an ancient ritual took place. Three times, the imperial insignia was offered to Li Yuan. Twice he refused it; then he accepted. Six days later, on the first day of a new cycle of the seasons, the new Emperor, known to history as Kao Tsu, proclaimed an amnesty or forgiveness for all his prisoners in celebration of the inauguration of the dynasty known as T'ang.

After placing his father on the throne, some say that Li Shih-min set out to consolidate his power and extend his rule. Marching eastward, he seized the city of Lo-yang, Yang-ti's eastern capital. He trapped the Sui nobles in their palace and held them there until they were forced to surrender. Leaving the city with some 50,000 prisoners, he set fire to the palace, which had been built, he explained, "with the life-blood of the people." Then he turned his attention to the South, to the region of Canton and the West River valley, and by 624 had brought it under his rule as well. Thus, in the short space of six years, the young conqueror had accomplished his goal: from Tibet to the sea, and from the Great Wall to the South China Sea, T'ang power was supreme. "Men of T'ang" the people of the South still call themselves, as if their history in fact had only begun at this moment of surrender to the Empire.

By this time, Kao Tsu was old and weak. The inheritance was destined for the eldest of his sons, and to prevent any argument about this fact, he ordered Li Shih-min to take command of the eastern territory from a post in Lo-yang. But the young conqueror was not ready to take second position in the empire he had created. On the fourth of July in 626, he hid himself in some bushes beside the gate to the palace, and when his brothers appeared, he shot them down with arrows. Then he took the throne himself. To future historians, he would be known as the glorious Emperor T'ai Tsung.

Thus the swashbuckling soldier took the reins of political power as well. Probably, once he had won this final goal, he turned his attention to problems of government which he felt were necessary if his empire was to hold together. He divided China into ten provinces, and prefectures and counties which could be efficiently overseen from the capital. He expanded and strengthened the civil service examinations, by which Chinese youths were encouraged to seek their futures in the bureaucracy. In this way, he hoped to continue to bring new blood into the government and to weaken the older aristocratic families, who might have divisive ambitions of their own. Now, every year, several thousand young men left their provincial homes and flocked to Ch'ang-an to prepare for these important tests. According to Confucius' view of man's nature, it was within each man's power to perfect himself by education, and the great source of China's moral and social strength, most emperors agreed, was in her students' mastery of the Classics, with their emphasis on social harmony and personal adjustment. T'ai Tsung probably concurred in this for reasons of policy at least, though at heart he was more moved by the Buddhist religion and did all he could to strengthen their establishments.

According to the doctrine expressed by Mencius, Confucius' great follower, "When one subdues men by force, they do not submit to him in heart . . . when one subdues men by virtue, they sincerely submit . . ." Following this principle, the Han code of laws was moderated in T'ang times. Formerly, heavy punishment was inflicted for any one of several hundred crimes. Now, only treason and murder were cause for the death penalty. Still, some customs which seem barbarous to us were maintained, but usually for reasons of Confucian logic. For lesser crimes, for instance, offenders might be sent into forced labor, or to exile, either briefly or for a lifetime, nearby or in the unhealthy South. In keeping with Confucius' emphasis on the bonds within a family, a man's sentence of exile might well be applied to his wife and children and to his descendants, until an imperial pardon might be arranged. Men close to the throne, like the poets and literary men who beguiled the emperors with their verse and were often commanded to speak their minds on political questions, were banished if their advice proved wrong. And yet, throughout the land, the people's courts and the judges who presided over them were subject to review by inspectors from Ch'ang-an every six months. For, according to Confucian doctrine, the higher a man's station in life, the greater his responsibility and the more drastic the punishment if he were guilty of a crime. The law in China was always principally a guideline, according to which justice was meted out by each judge in accord with his view of the situation. Only in Ch'in China, eight centuries before, had it been taken as basic that even judges are subject to personal enthusiasms, and that safety for all is better obtained by laws which ride above personalities.

From a military point of view, one of T'ai Tsung's great achievements was pushing back the eastern Turks and so once more making travel safe over the northern route. After one decisive battle, T'ai Tsung's armies chased the remnants of that horde north into the Gobi Desert. A fog suddenly descended, and the Turkish army, its herds of camels, cattle and horses, were captured and destroyed. The Khan himself was taken prisoner and sent to Ch'ang-an, where he was put to work in the imperial stables.

In 634, T'ai Tsung ordered a new section of the palace to be erected, which he called the Palace of Great Brightness. Here, he reigned for fifteen years before retiring to the Kingfisher Blue Palace in the Nan-shan mountains to the south of his city. There, in 649, he died.

In the centuries that followed T'ai Tsung's reign, the arts—sculpture, architecture, bronzework and gold, poetry, music and glazed ceramics—

flowered in China with new richness. During the brilliant middle and late years of the Dynasty, T'ang power reached from the eastern sea westward beyond India, where her emissaries met men of the Byzantine Empire. From them, they learned what the Han had known centuries before: that to the west was a great civilization, as old as their own, but now crumbled into fragments.

For at this time all Europe lay in ruin and abandon. The broad, paved roads and columned cities of the Roman Empire had become campgrounds for the bands of warriors who had overrun them. The rich culture of the old Classical world—its sculpture and painting, its philosophy and science— were unknown to these "barbarians," who only slowly learned to reach out toward them. Lost to Europe, Classical civilization survived only at the eastern end of the Mediterranean, in the libraries and academies of Constantinople, capital of Byzantium.

But the T'ang rulers came to power after no such radical break in continuity. In spite of the social breakdown which had followed the Chou and Han Dynasties, the T'ang emperors considered themselves rooted in the ancient past of their empire, inheritors of the Mandate of Heaven down the line from the god-men of prehistory. So, in spite of occasional, devastating interruptions during the three-hundred-year T'ang rule, the fundamental forms of government and society remained much the same as those evolved long before.

Chapter VII The Great City

Beyond the frontiers lie the hard winters and the raging winds ...
We entered the land of the Huns and subdued them in their desert strongholds ..
The soldiers of Han returned in triumph ...
And on the altar of heaven we sang our victory.

(LI SHIH-MIN, *later Emperor T'ai Tsung*)

Man of the frontier, trained to the surge of battles in the northern steppes, conqueror yet friend of any who came in friendship, Li Shih-min stamped the early part of the T'ang Dynasty with his own personality. His experiences in outlying lands led him to be generous toward other peoples, concerned for their well-being, protective of their ideas. Or at least so his historians, who chronicled his reign with lavish praises, have painted him as being. Once, for example, he returned a tribute-gift of a number of young slaves because he felt it was wrong to take them from

74

their parents. His courtiers were told to address the Dragon Throne not in "frothy and flowery style, which is useless," but to be frank and straightforward and get to the point. So, it seems, were his artists instructed. One or a number of them, for instance, made stone portraits of his beloved Turkish horses—stocky creatures who had survived with him the terrible battles of his youth. A number of these relief sculptures still exist. Each shows a steed in heavy profile. One is named "Autumn Dew." Trustingly, it stands stock still while one of T'ai Tsung's generals extracts an arrow from its chest.

Yet like the boy he still was, the Emperor loved the trappings of luxury too. His favorite suit of armor had been brought to him from Korea. It was a costume of golden lacquer on which a panorama of mountains had been delicately engraved. In this shining jacket, moving with haughty dignity through the stiff ceremonies of the Palace of Great Brightness, Li Shih-min must have felt that he was, indeed, the Son of the Heavens. At his hip rode a sword with jeweled hilt and golden shaft, carried in a sheath of tough sharkskin from the southern seas. At hand was his ceremonial bow, which partook of the power of the sky itself: as lightning flashed from the clouds, so might Li Shih-min's arrow speed out, direct and destroying.

There is a painting in the collection of the Nationalist Chinese peoples now headquartered on Taiwan, which, though it was done after his lifetime, shows T'ai Tsung as he may well have looked. Like most Chinese men in the flush of youth, he is stocky and his round face is unlined. Clever black eyes stare out eagerly from beneath eyebrows as slanted as crows' wings. He wears a wispy mustache, and his beard juts forward in a breezy curve. His loose gown of golden silk is embroidered with the imperial pattern: a roundel of sweeping clouds in which dances a dragon, twisting its head backward, its tail and limbs thrashing. He stands with his hands looped into his embroidered belt, his black felt boots widely planted, gazing into the distance as if upon far-off plains, mountains rising toward a cold sky, and passes where enemy horsemen hide. He is, indeed, the vigorous son of a vigorous race and a benevolent heaven.

By his hand, North and East had fallen. Now by his hand the great capital city of the Sui must be made into a fitting capital for the T'ang, just as, long before, the Han Emperors had dreamed of doing. "The Emperor planned here a base of imperial power to endure a hundred

Clothed in the heavy felt boots and thick costume of the northern frontier and armed with a quiver full of arrows, one of T'ai Tsung's generals here draws an enemy arrow from the chest of one of his sovereign's beloved warhorses. A series of "portraits" of these stocky, thick-muscled beasts was made at the command of the Emperor. A number of them have survived, to show us how steeds and soldiers were saddled and armed, and also with what mastery the T'ang artists worked.

thousand years," wrote the Han chronicler; yet by T'ai Tsung's time, nothing remained of that dream but a pile of stones.

Nobody knows why the Chinese elected to build their cities of such ephemeral materials: earthen walls that heavy rains could melt; wooden shacks and roofs that the least flame could consume; and the whole so vulnerable to the attacks of men that, repeatedly, they were overrun by hordes from the north or rebels from within. Then these marauders spared nothing and later boasted their horses could gallop over the ruins without stumbling. Little wonder that the later Chinese scholars treasured those few objects that had escaped the holocaust—a creamy bowl, for instance, or a fragment of silk bearing the brushwork of a famous artist. "The T'ang plate, the Confucian tripod are eternal things . . ." wrote a T'ang poet. Eternal or not, they are all we have—together with the words of poets and historians—to reconstruct T'ai Tsung's Ch'ang-an in our imagination, for in reality there remains of it only the two pagodas and a stretch of land.

Two million people are thought to have lived in and just surrounding T'ang Ch'ang-an. As T'ai Tsung approached his great city along the royal road from the south, between fields of millet stretching as far as his eye could see and tended by some of those two million, bending over the furrows, averting their gaze from his august presence, he would have sensed in the distance the hum and bustle of those who lived within the city walls— shopkeepers and artisans, slaves and bureaucrats, dancing girls and poets.

As he drew near, he would have caught sight of the five-portaled Gate of Brilliant Virtue, whose columns were lacquered a flaming vermilion. Beyond the gate, he could have looked down a broad, tree-shaded avenue which terminated, five miles off, in another set of vermilion gates, those of the official Palace City. Further on, extending into the Imperial Park, lay his own private residence, the Palace of Great Brightness, with its flamboyant Gate of the Vermilion Phoenix.

On either side of the long avenue which bifurcated the city, lay the swarming, walled-in wards of T'ai Tsung's children, the common people. These people lived in one-storied wooden houses, each with its tiny plot of enclosed garden, reflecting the ancient architectural layout of the farmer's compound, with its kitchen garden and shed for livestock. Now daughters and sons, and their families in time, often crowded into the same expandable living quarters, generations supporting and honoring one another according to Confucian rules. During the day, a bustle of activity went on here. Men in blue or black cotton jackets and trousers went forth to work; women with wicker baskets over their arms set out to pick over the wares at market. But at dusk a big gong was struck, and when darkness fell, silence also fell upon the residential quarters. No one was allowed to leave his ward. Anyone found away from home was liable to seventy lashes of the whip. All night, mounted guards patrolled the streets. At last, at dawn, the great drums rolled again, and one by one, the city gates were swung open and also the lesser gates of the wards.

Beyond the residential wards, also to the right and left of the main avenue, lay the markets. On the east, or right, was the center for big firms doing business in grain, timber, spices and other products, most of which came up by canal from the Yangtze basin and the farther south seaport of Canton. Here a new houseowner might search among barge-loads of furniture made of the spotted bamboo, the aromatic rosewoods and laurel of the South. Perfumers, cooks and medical men might come here to find, wholesale, the sweet-smelling herbs and spices of the southern isles— frankincense and cloves, patchouli and musk from the jungles of south China and beyond.

An even more colorful part of the city may have been the western or left-hand market. For here it was that camel caravans terminated after the overland march from the Indies. Bells jangling, leather harnesses slapping, these awkward beasts knelt down like ocean boats beaching, to let their drivers unload bales of wares which had crossed the icy peaks and ghost-ridden deserts. The bales were distributed to various arcades, for each product had its special district within the market. Syrian glass in skyblue hues, cups made of ostrich eggs from Samarkand, silver ewers with animal-head spouts from the smithies of Persia—these were laid out in the arcade. In the cloth market were materials from the looms of all the known world, exchanged for bolts of Chinese silk and taffeta destined for those same far-flung markets. Printed cotton came from Java and Bali, dyed in suc-culent vegetable tones—lavender, soft green, burnt red. From other Indo-chinese looms came a silk dyed the color of "sunrise clouds of morning." Felt was shipped down by the tribesmen of the steppes, made of animal hair beaten into mats and dyed scarlet or snow white. There were carpets too, woven in Syrian workshops, of dark red wools adorned with drifts of

This very camel could have walked in Ch'ang-an. On his saddle, adorned with a monster-mask, he carries a side of meat, a water flask and a portable bamboo bed. Below, five musicians gaily blow pipes and whistles from the backs of their horses.

In the T'ang Dynasty the arts of
sculpture and metalwork flourished, and for the palace nobles,
gorgeous jewels, costumes and
decorations were turned out. Few
of these remain today. This T'ang
(or perhaps slightly earlier) lion,
rearing and growling, once
guarded the way to a tomb or important building. Some T'ang
princess may have possessed this
intricate, proud golden phoenix,
and her warrior husband, the silver placque showing a silhouetted
horse, adorned and prancing.

A

B

C

flowers. And there were even rarer cloths, for no one but residents of the Court of the Bright Sun, the women's quarters of the palace: a cinnamon-gold material, for instance, woven with filaments from a musselshell which inhabits the Indian Ocean and the Persian Gulf. About this fabulous cloth, the Chinese wove legends, saying it was harvested by dragon-weavers from the backs of sheep who live beneath the waves.

Strange beasts, alive, were brought to please T'ai Tsung. Two years after he ascended the throne, a lion was uncrated in the marketplace, sent to him as a gift from far-off Samarkand. "It glares its eyes, and lightning flashes,/ It vents its voice, and thunder echoes . . ." wrote a poet who observed it, tearing at its wooden bars, roaring with a voice as deep, people said, as the voice of Buddha when he taught his lesson to the world. Milder beasts were brought in too: green peacocks, and hawks with their wiry throats encased in embroidered silk collars, and, at least once during the T'ang Dynasty, a real "Kalavinka" bird, which, according to legend, came from the snowy peaks of India and sang "while still in the egg," in a voice of unsurpassed sweetness teaching Buddha's lesson that the universal is as ephemeral as a song. One modern scholar identifies this bird with the blue-black Drongo, a real-life song-bird with sweeping tailfeathers from the jungles of Java, but to the merchants and princes of T'ang, its actual identity was of little importance next to the fact that it came from far away, and in its strangeness, seemed to possess magic powers.

Elsewhere were the dark, fragrant cubicles of magicians and medicine men. They offered orchids from the south, good for the bites of venomous insects, and python bile for malaria, and dragons' bones for weakness. Mushrooms and various roots and herbs, beeswax and human hair, crushed spiders and tiger meat—strange combinations of substances from near and far were ground up here and offered as cures for toothaches, melancholia or grave illness, whether of the farmer or of the Son of Heaven himself.

There were dealers in gold—gold dust, and gold leaf to cover the statues of Buddha in the temples, and miniscule granules of gold for the earrings and bracelets of T'ai Tsung's women—and dealers in pearls, and jade white as moonlight or green as the southern forests, and opals and malachite.

Picking among these crowded stalls, a crowd as colorful and varied as the wares themselves could be seen during the years of T'ang ascendancy. Westerners from near the Mediterranean shores, with curly hair and blue eyes, rubbed shoulders with Hindus in one-shouldered robes, their chests draped with heavy strings of gems. Turbaned and bearded Arabs thrust their way through the crowd, jostling visitors from Japan, curious, diminutive people who were dealers in writing brushes and inlaid ivory boxes, or sometimes just tourists from that land emerging into the light of civilization, eager to copy the ways of their sophisticated neighbor across the Yellow Sea. All these types can be seen today, almost with the same cheerful vitality they possessed in life, in the clay figurines which, according to T'ang custom, were put into graves to keep the dead company. Here we can see T'ang tumblers and jugglers showing their muscles, T'ang dancers lifting their long sleeves, men of the distant steppes with hooked noses and eagle eyes and others whose appearance must have startled and then inspired the sculptor to catch them forever in clay—like a hunchbacked street-vendor, carrying his wares in a heavy sack.

Here and there, pushing their way between these vendors and the camels and horses, went the women of Ch'ang-an, some in silk and jewels, borne by their slaves in palanquins, their foreheads stylishly aglow with golden powder, and others, their faces deeply lined by winter winds and the harsh dusts of summer, looking for simple food to keep their families alive. For the poor, rice and eggs, a bit of dry fish, a handful of vegetables sufficed. But for the tables of the rich, there were baskets of deers' tongues and seahorses, edible snakes, oysters, little figurines of sugar and ginger for the children, and heaps of magnificent fruit: peaches and melons, each one wrapped and packed in a little bamboo box to keep it from bruising, and tangerines of two kinds, "sweetpeel" and "sourpeel."

When their labors were over—if they ever ended—both rich and poor might join in Ch'ang-an in a park which lay at the southeast corner of the city. The Serpentine was a place of winding paths and small lakes crossed by marble bridges, of gardens and groves of trees and of wood pavilions for talking, or writing poetry, or simply resting to enjoy the cool.

But beyond this graceful spot, there were few other public pleasures for the people, none of those theaters or baths or circuses which the Emperors of Rome and Byzantium offered their populace. The Chinese people were not considered citizens of a political organization within which they could claim certain rights; they were no more than the children of the Emperor, living in his city at his invitation. "The two capitals, Ch'ang-an and

B

C

Little clay figures were placed in T'ang tombs, perhaps to keep the dead person company in his next life, and to remind him of the sights and sounds of this one. Here are a bullock pulling a wagon, a court musician plucking her mandolin-like instrument, and a bearded peddler toting his heavy box of wares through the city streets.

Lo-yang, are first and foremost the mansions of the Emperor." So read a T'ang edict of 731.

Within his mansion, the Ta Ming Palace, T'ai Tsung and his followers lived a life of complex pageantry, for he was, at once, father of his people, head of the Imperial House, first farmer of the land, and symbolic Son of Heaven. The rituals to which he must lend his presence were many. One, which he performed shortly after coming to the throne, was called "Opening the Eyes of the Buddha." Probably, he was ceremoniously presented with a brush and directed in painting in the eyes of a sacred statue. He had constant duties to fulfill to the imperial ancestors, too, visiting their graves scattered throughout the plains and mountains around the city, carrying on sacrifices to win over their support.

He had civic duties as well, presiding at meetings of the court where government problems were presented and discussed and foreign ambassadors introduced. These assemblies took place at the break of dawn, just after the red-hatted guards of the Palace City had given their daybreak cry and swung open the big doors. No one was allowed to refuse the imperial summons or to be late, so to be on the safe side, many lesser officials came while it was still night and stood shivering, waiting for the call.

At Ch'ang-an—a full foot of snow
A levee at dawn, to bestow congratulations on the Emperor . . .
I waited for the summons within the Triple Hall
My hair and beard were frozen and covered with icicles;
My coat and robe—chilly like water . . .

Within, wrapped in state robes embroidered with dragons, motionless upon the Dragon Throne, the Emperor waited. His very presence shed a magic power within the chamber. Usually, he sat in silence, letting his lesser courtiers conduct the business of the day. When he left the sacred enclosure, it was as if a ghostly wind swept down the street: no commoner was allowed to look at his person. Some emperors, in fact, spent almost their whole lives within the confines of their palace, moving from place to place only through special roadways covered over from view. Like the polar star around which the cosmos turned, the Emperor was the very center and ridgepole of the world.

And yet when his imperial duties were over, within his private quarters protected from curious eyes and from those who might want to do him

84

harm, the Emperor enjoyed sumptuous pleasures. There were banquets for two hundred guests. If T'ai Tsung commanded, his Indian or Turkestan musicians would bow forth to enchant the company with their twining and untwining melodies, filled with longing or the rhythms of battle. To the sound of their flutes and oboes, their gongs and drums and stringed instruments, dancing boys and girls performed. Perhaps T'ai Tsung would call for the "Kalavinka" dance. Then, with wings attached to their backs and flower garlands in their hair, the boys and girls would leap and turn while they played little finger cymbals tinkling as the mysterious bird's voice. Or he might prefer the "Western Prancing Dance." Then, with their long belts flying like manes, the dancers would crouch and whirl as if they had turned into the "supernatural" horses of the Central Asian steppe. Or perhaps the Emperor might command a performance by one of his solo artists, like Eldest Sister Kung, who was famous for moving her arms so gracefully that she reminded the company of characters brushed in ink.

Next morning, T'ai Tsung might ride out upon one of his horses into the Imperial Park behind the Palace City. There was room in those miles of natural forest for hunts, or for casual explorations. Beside the ruins of the old Han capital, T'ai Tsung might dismount to meditate about other Sons of Heaven before him who had vanished now into legend. Later he might spend an hour at the imperial archery range, or playing ball in the imperial courts. His companions were members of his family, and the aristocratic old families, some of whom could trace their lineage back to the Chou period. These people too lived in splendor, often wholly supported by the court out of taxes and tribute monies. One official in Ch'ang-an had three thousand servants working for him. Another had a "self raining" pavilion on his roof to keep the house cool in summer.

Even so, surrounded by luxuries from the world's coffers, it seems that T'ai Tsung did not lose his frontiersman's curiosity about ideas and people from far away. In 635, a monk from the west came to his court to preach a certain Christian doctrine. T'ai Tsung listened attentively to this man's explanations and then issued a judgment which would be considered liberal even today: "The Way has more than one name," he declared. "Doctrines differ in different lands. O Lo Pen, a man of great virtue, has brought his images and books from afar to present them in our capital. After studying his principles, we find that they stress what is good and important. Let it be preached freely in Our Empire." So O Lo Pen was permitted to build and

Here are two high-born women of the T'ang era, stolidly built yet graceful, dressed in thick silk robes, with their hair in heavy, upswept coils. They are bearing gifts, perhaps to the Emperor in one of the elaborate palace rituals.

preach within a Nestorian church, upon whose altar stood a Cross of Christianity.

Three years later, an ambassador from the Persian court came to T'ai Tsung. In their westward march, the Turks had conquered the old Sassanian armies, and the deposed Emperor wished to enlist T'ai Tsung's help to turn them back. The Chinese Emperor was not convinced that he should send his forces so far beyond the Wall, but he invited the Sassanian refugees to live out their lives in Ch'ang-an and to set up their own temples, which were dedicated to the Zoroastrian god of light, Ahura Mazda.

Thus the world pressed close to the court of T'ai Tsung. One traveler came to tell him about the great city then reigning over the western world. "Fu Lin," he said, speaking of Constantinople, "is situated on the Western Sea. The walls of the city are of stone. In the Imperial Palace is a human figure of gold which marks the hours by striking bells. The buildings are decorated with glass and crystal, gold, ivory and rare woods . . ." He described the inhabitants of this great city, too, Ch'ang-an's only rival in time and splendor. "The men wear their hair cut short and are clothed in embroidered robes which leave the right arm bare. The women wear their hair in the form of a crown . . . On the seventh day, no work is done . . ."

The colorful, international ambiance of T'ai Tsung's court claimed, however, one unhappy victim. The Emperor's son, crown prince of the realm, was consumed by enthusiasm for the life of a Turk. He had a felt tent set up in the Imperial Park, and there he lived, wearing Turkish robes, eating game roasted over a bonfire, amusing himself with Turkish comrades. Soon it became clear to T'ai Tsung that the boy's fancy had gone beyond the bounds of reason and that he had neither the wish nor the force to govern the Central Kingdom. So, decisively, T'ai Tsung exiled his son to the south of China where he died, perhaps out of longing for his beloved north. A new crown prince was brought forward. Later, after T'ai Tsung's death, he became Emperor Kao Tsung.

When T'ai Tsung had been ten years upon the throne, he selected a lovely fourteen-year-old girl named Wu Chao, whom he called Beauty Wu, to join his large company of concubines. After his death in 649, Wu and all the other women of his harem were sent off to a Buddhist convent to spend the rest of their lives in prayer and meditation. But Wu Chao was young and ambitious, and having once tasted worldly pleasures near the Dragon

Throne, was in no mood to bury herself in tedious convent life. Soon, she managed to attract the attention of the new Emperor, and with the connivance of his Empress, who hoped to have an accomplice in certain of her plans, convinced him to take her back to the palace. Once there, she gradually took on more power for herself until she conspired to oust the real Empress from her position. In the year 655, on the twelfth day of December, the entire court, including wives of the officials, assembled to pay her honor and to recognize her claim to the Dragon Throne, going back through the generations of imperial ancestors, to the god-men of antiquity. Empress Wu may well have had the dainty face, with small sharp features and plucked eyebrows which are portrayed in later paintings of her imperial person, but she must have borne herself with steely vigor to have carried off a ceremony so against the Confucian grain: no woman in Chinese history had claimed the official powers of Heaven and worn upon her back the ceremonial robes embroidered, in gold and vermilion threads, with the mystic design of dragons and heavenly clouds.

In her rise to such eminence, Wu had committed fearful crimes. The former Empress and another of Kao Tsung's favorites she had banished to a desolate corner of the Palace City where, forgotten and half starved, they languished in a cell. One day, they happened to attract the attention of a passerby, who carried the news of their plight to Kao Tsung. When he complained to Wu, she flew into a rage, ordered the unfortunate women thrown into a vat, decapitated and cut into pieces.

Soon, however, their ghosts would not let her rest. Trailing their wretched presences through her dreams, the women haunted her, crying out and accusing her of crimes she well knew she had committed. Magicians were called to try to chase away the spirits, but no potions or spells worked. Eventually, Empress Wu had to leave the Palace of Great Brightness altogether, with its chambers full of echoes and its outlying dungeon pits. She moved the entire court and government two hundred miles east, to Loyang. Here, for the better part of half a century, she ruled in easier splendor.

During her long reign, trade between China and the West flourished and a number of southern towns, like Canton and Hangchow, came into new prominence. These rambling cities, sprawling around natural harbors, were never so rigidly laid out or supervised as the historic cities of the North. Along the quays and jetties which received two-hundred-foot boats from across the China seas, a restless jumble of foreigners came to buy and sell.

Sleek-bodied, delicate men of the south—Khmers and Javanese, Singhalese and Hindus—traded their tales of adventure at sea. Bit by bit, China's economic and spiritual center began to shift toward the South and in future centuries, these southern centers would in fact become more populous and active than the old northern meeting places of tribesmen and descendants of the Chou, which lay dangerously open to attack from the steppes. In reverse, however, Wu also encouraged the sons of farming families in the South to move north and submit to the civil service examinations. This way, she hoped, like many other emperors, to balance North against South, aristocracy against new power, to maintain a stability in the land making civil rebellion unlikely.

Perhaps to soothe her conscience, Wu became an ardent Buddhist and built a great number of temples with attached hospitals for the poor. Her tastes in architecture were grandiose. Within her own palace, a voluminous Hall of Light was set aside for special ceremonies. In nine tall bronze holders, tapers shed their dancing light. In the middle of the hall, a lofty iron pillar supported a bronze ball that cast a thousand reflections. This represented the Celestial Axis, axis of the universe, around which Empress Wu's domain yearly revolved.

Only a few years ago, reports from Communist China announced the discovery of a tomb belonging to a princess Yung-tai, who lived during the reign of Empress Wu. Grave robbers had taken away all the gold and silver ornaments which once lay heaped about her bier. But painted upon the walls of the tomb, a procession of regal women still marched in stately array, dressed in heavy robes, holding fans and combs and mirrors. They are the perfect blooms of the early T'ang period: dignified, regal and erect, their hair dressed in heavy upswept rolls, their faces archly made-up to emphasize their wide eyes and smooth brows. The self-confident, rhythmic pace of a young culture in control of its power: this is the mark of T'ang culture in its early flowering.

Chapter VIII   The Sun at its Zenith

. . . good fortune falls on the gold-pillared gateway . . .
The prophecies of T'ai Tsung are supreme,
The empire is firmly established and reaches the sky!

(TU FU)

Not until the age of 81, in 705, was Empress Wu deposed, and soon afterward she died. Though the fact that a woman held the Dragon Throne never sat well with the traditional Confucians, actually she had ruled with decisiveness and left behind a stable empire.

Seven years after her death, her grandson ascended the throne, to reign for nearly half a century. At the end, he would leave a heritage of tragedy, but his life until that turning point spanned the most glorious years of the dynasty, a flowering of painting and poetry and a period of peace for most of his children. He was to be known in history as Emperor Hsüan-tsung, but to the poets by his nickname, Ming Huang, the "Brilliant" Emperor. There exists a portrait which shows Ming Huang seated on a jewel-studded chair whose legs are carved like petals and clouds. He is very paunchy; his eyes are mere curves of light in his jowly face. But his slender fingers are sensitive, and he leans forward, turning a kindly gaze on the beholder.

In 713, Ming Huang celebrated his first New Year in power. From earliest antiquity, the people of China had celebrated this holiday on the night of the full moon of the first month of the year, marking the turn of the seasons away from winter toward the softer evenings of spring. At first, the agricultural peoples probably heralded this night with bonfires and processions of priests carrying torches. But sometime during the troubled centuries after the Han when there was much exchange with the west, a more fanciful symbol of the occasion was introduced: a "fire tree," or tree of lamps. As our Christmas Tree evolved from a simple fir into the emblem of celebration we know today, so the idea of a lamp tree became more elaborate. For his festival of lights, Ming Huang commanded an immense wooden wheel to be built just outside the walls of his Palace City, where all the people of Ch'ang-an could gather. On this scaffold, fifty thousand tiny bowls were hung, and in each one danced a tongue of flame. A thousand women, with flowers woven into their black hair, tended this light wheel, which flickered against the night like a galaxy come down to earth.

Upon the wall of his enclave, Ming Huang stood with his arm around his aged father, gazing over the crowds of rejoicing people and the flamboyant turn of stars he had provided for them. Now upon his own shoulders rested the responsibility for the coming of spring to the Central Kingdom. His, now, was the task of setting the sacred plow to the furrow, of tending the holy graves, of shepherding his children through the paces of their lives.

Much of what we know of the splendor of Ming Huang's reign comes from a source across the seas. In 756, the year before Ming Huang's final abdication, the Emperor of Japan died. In his honor, his widow presented all the gifts and tribute he had accumulated in his lifetime to a Buddhist temple in the Japanese city of Nara. Chests upon chests of these objects were stacked by the Buddhist monks in a simple log building in a grove of trees, sealed and not publicly reopened until this century. There, like the manuscripts of Tun-huang, they slept through the centuries that obliterated the arts of T'ang from the Central Kingdom. In one respect, the Shoso-in treasures were even more representative of Imperial T'ang style than those at Tun-huang, for they were products of the finest imperial workshops, destined for the imperial treasuries. Tun-huang, though an important crossroads between China and the West, was still never more than a provincial waystop where artists of the second rank worked, far from the stylistic impulses of the capital. Thus, in the coffers of the Shoso-in lay a kaleidoscope of the kind of goods Ming Huang and his neighbor, Emperor Shomu, actually held in their hands.

Shomu's inlaid ivory gameboard is here, and a lute painted with joyful scenes of musicians. Embroidered slippers for his feet, and textiles whose delicacy tells of the skill of imperial weavers in the eighth century. Some are woven in elaborate, twining patterns of lotus and animal forms. Others are printed, or painted, or dyed. On one, now discolored with age, brown deer stand beneath sprays of browned wisteria. There are boxes, too, of the rare drugs men of this time took to lift their spirits—epsom salts, powdered rhinoceros horn and dragons' bones. In case these failed to work their magic, Shomu possessed a Taoist "wish-fulfilling wand," made of a strip of colored horn, inlaid with blue lapis. With this, he might succeed in turning plain water into the Elixir of Immortality.

From the west, beyond China, had come other gifts: Persian fabrics woven with leaping horses and griffins; a sky-blue glass bowl, set by an imaginative silversmith into a shining base; a Turkish Khan's belt, heavy with lumps of lapis lazuli; carpets of scarlet felt from Central Asia.

Nor was the Shoso-in the only source in Japan from which modern scholars have learned what Ming Huang's palaces looked like. For during the years of his reign, while trade westward expanded then withered according to the fortunes of the tribes north of the wall, Chinese ideas and arts poured steadily into Japan. Her shores were close enough to China's mainland to permit easy travel, first via Korea and later, over the sea between Nagasaki and the southern ports. Thus in fact, Japan was the easternmost land into which Buddhist ideas and art could spread, and there, as if in a cul-de-sac, they have been preserved in countless temples and temple treasuries.

Before Buddhism found its way into Japan, the country was held in the grip of a relatively primitive religion called Shinto, which was, in effect, a way of explaining the violent and sudden catastrophes—typhoons and earthquakes—that so frequently struck this small island-country. The chief Shinto deity was a kindly sun goddess who bathed the rice fields in her warm rays. But the rest of creation, the Shinto people believed, was alive with evil spirits, leaping in the bonfire, sleeping in the muddy fields, hiding, even, in the carpenter's materials, ready to twist and make his house fall down if he failed to perform the required sacrifices or to handle his saw and hammer with care. The Buddhism that found its way into this anxious country had changed a great deal since the birth of gentle Siddhartha in his Himalayan village a thousand years earlier. As the Buddhist tales had filtered eastward through China, they had taken on many new saints and heroes, among whom Buddha himself was worshipped as a supreme god. In Japan, the Shinto demons and spirits quickly found their own niches around Buddha.

After the T'ang rule was established, with Ch'ang-an its rich and cosmopolitan religious center, many Japanese observers came to visit it, and from China, Buddhist missionaries and artists went forth to proselytize. So admiring of their more advanced neighbors were the Japanese emperors that, in the year 710, five years after the death of Empress Wu and two years before her grandson took the throne, the Japanese city of Nara was laid out along the lines of Ch'ang-an, only smaller. Based on a grid of broad avenues enlivened with streams and feathery gardens, Nara and the later city of Kyoto give us some general idea of how Ch'ang-an looked to the people who thronged its streets.

Heart of the social and religious life of Nara was a great temple complex which included a wide enclosure, lined with cells for monks and pilgrims, surrounding a main shrine at the center. The temple of Horyuji is almost the only example left in the world today which shows us how the imperial carpenters of the T'ang and Nara periods worked. Upon slender wood poles, intricately joined, they raised up elaborate roofs which lie so heavily thatched or tiled they seem like the folded wings of ponderous birds, gracefully turned up at the corners. The columns, ceilings and walls were tiled, or brightly painted—red, blue, green and gold—as if it were the architect's dream to "outdazzle the sun." So a Chinese poet wrote of a temple with its shining bronze bells, its silken banners floating on the lightest breeze, its carved wooden panels decorated with vines and trailing clouds. Along the walls of the buildings, fresh flowers bloomed in wooden boxes, tame deer and doves came to feed from the hands of visitors, and from mysterious recesses overhead, the tinkle of jade wind-chimes sounded, like the breathing of wind-spirits.

These temples were, in the time of Ming Huang and the other T'ang rulers, small cities unto themselves. Courtyards led into long galleries where libraries and meditation halls received the scholarly-minded. Dormitories and hospitals were available for the poor and hungry, men without homes and orphans in need of nursing. For the wandering pilgrim, each temple had its special holy relic to be adored: one famous monastery in China had a silver harp on which, it was believed, 84,000 notes could be played, each one with the power to cure one of the worldly passions. A particular temple in Ch'ang-an possessed as its greatest treasure one of the Buddha's teeth; another had a bit of the Buddha's skull with a few white hairs still attached to its crown; another in Ch'ang-an claimed to have a bone of the great Indian Buddhist king Asoka. Famous works of art were displayed in the temples too: the Temple of the Holy Flower in Ch'ang-an owned a Buddhist figure of brass which had been brought from the oasis of Khotan; upon the walls of this temple were paintings which the monk-caretakers said had been created by supernatural spirits.

During Ming Huang's reign, Chinese artists in Japan taught the Japanese their methods of casting and shaping bronze and carving wood figures. These T'ang-style Japanese Buddhas are heavy and stolid, often clothed in the rich court jewelry and scarves of the imperial court. Beside them, in the Japanese shrines, the old Shinto demons stride forward, hair flying, baring their teeth and shaking their fists.

There are fragments of T'ang-style painting still to be seen in Japan today, as well. In the Shoso-in are several screens painted by Chinese artists, showing plump court ladies in thick, bright wrappers, gossiping beneath the branches of trees that perhaps shaded the Serpentine Park in Ch'ang-an.

Most of the painters of Ming Huang's time used a brush style which had been invented long before in India. Called the "iron wire" line, this tense, decisive way of drawing with the brush was carried into China by Buddhist artists working along the caravan trails, in places like Tun-huang. This style, apparently, was also used in official works made for the imperial family, for it is in the "iron wire" line that Princess Yang-ti of the court of Empress Wu was depicted.

Some say it was a master of Ming Huang's time named Wu Tao-tzu who invented a different style, which quickly became popular and led eventually to the supreme invention of Chinese painters, the landscape scroll. The new manner bore the descriptive name "orchid petal line." Bending, flowing and twisting, it varied in thickness and blackness and was a line which seemed

晉武帝司馬炎

Painting, as well as the other arts flourished in T'ang Dynasty workshops.
Chinese painters worked on paper or silk, with a soft brush dipped into inks
or watercolors. This magnificently robed and hatted being is an earlier Emperor, by a T'ang artist.

Only a few years ago, this humped mound in China was excavated by Communist archaeologists and found to contain the tomb of a T'ang Dynasty princess, Yang-ti. Along the walls were paintings of her elegantly dressed court attendants.

B

to live and breathe as the traditional "iron wire" line did not. Perhaps it was a line more expressive of Taoist ideas. "The spirit lives in the point of the brush," wrote a Chinese critic of this new style. The painted line, in fact, according to these Chinese artists, had a magic power to make living beings react in certain ways. "In the beginning were sorcerers," wrote a scholar. "Later there were painters in the spirit of Tao." Thus a line drawn in ink in the orchid petal manner seemed to hold a charge of energy which could be received by one who was in an appreciative mood, giving him a sense of the rhythms of the universe itself.

Or it may have been another master of Ming Huang's court, Wang Wei, who invented the new style. "In his paintings are his poems," it was said of Wang Wei, who wrote poetry as well, "and in his poems are his paintings." A devout Buddhist yet steeped in Taoist ideas, Wang Wei, like most of his colleagues, looked to nature, to the spiny hills and splashing water of his environment, rather than to the muscles and bones of the human figure, for his subject. "To exert oneself with strange mountains and seas," he wrote of his art, "with green forests and the scary winds, with the foaming waters and the rushing cascades—how wonderful! Such is the joy of painting!"

Ming Huang, it was said, once asked Wu Tao-tzu to make sketches of a river and then combine them into a long painting to cover the walls of one of his audience chambers. The painter returned from a day's ramble along the riverbank empty-handed. "I have it all in my heart," he explained to his imperial patron and then dashed off the entire panorama in a single day, in a cascading series of ink splashes. Meanwhile, another painter commissioned to do the same scene in the old, official style spent a full month carefully outlining his scene upon the wall, combining a delicate tracery of iron-wire lines with golden washes. "Each kind of painting is perfect in its own way," said Ming Huang, showing himself to be as generous in esthetic matters as old T'ai Tsung had been in religious ones.

After the T'ang Dynasty, for centuries even until the present time, each Chinese painter has adopted one or the other style as his particular way of working. Either he continued to employ the iron-wire line and turned out images of scenes around the imperial court, or luxurious flowers, or plump birds on a branch. Or he worked in ink, in a "broken" style, letting his brush dash here and there in an attempt to catch the very swing, break, and ripple of nature. For example, as T'ai Tsung had done before him, Ming Huang commanded an artist to make portraits, only this time in iron-wire painting, of his beloved warhorses. These, "Flying Yellow," "Night Lightning," "Drifting Cloud," and others, had been trained to lift their hooves and prance when certain military airs were played. Later, after Ming Huang came to a tragic end, his stables were broken up and the famous dancing horses scattered here and there in other properties throughout the country. Even so, whenever one of the horses heard the music of drums and pipes, he would lift his hooves again and dance, remembering the stables of the Son of Heaven. Music and painting too, the Chinese recognized, had powers not always understood by men, to make men and beasts react in certain ways. Wu Tao-tzu, it was said, once painted a picture of the Buddhist hell in his wild manner which was so frightening that all the butchers of Ch'ang-an set down their knives and vowed never to slaughter another beast.

As early as the sixth century A.D., a famous Chinese artist named Hsieh Ho had put forward "Six Principles" which defined the art of painting forever after in China. Of these, the most important were to catch the "life breath" of the subject, as Wu Tao-tzu did, and, as others more in the Confucian stream attempted, to copy works of the past in order to preserve them for the future. Only a very few original T'ang paintings are left, but the styles of the great masters of the period have been preserved in later copies made by artists and even emperors of the Sung and Ming periods, thanks to the recommendations of Hsieh Ho, who thought it better to copy antiquity than to strike out in new directions.

Thanks, too, to the preservers of past achievements, the rich output of the poets of Ming Huang's time has been passed down to our own. In earliest antiquity, the Chinese peasant had given voice to feelings which, eventually, the official poets made it their task to record. Calling on the elements—wind, storm and sunlight—the farmer sang songs to propel him through his cycles of work and repose.

> *Weave your linen no longer! Go to the marketplace!*
> *Dance! Dance!*
> *Withered leaves! Withered leaves! The wind will come and blow upon you!*

Stooping and pulling, digging and lifting to coax the millet out of the fields, the peasant felt these and a thousand other folkchants rise to his lips, half melody, half message to the gods. Like the landscapes of Wu Tao-tzu, these verses forged forward through flashes of brilliant description:

99

Most paintings of the T'ang Dynasty were lost in flames or the desolation which followed wars, but some masterpieces of the time were preserved, in essence, in copies made by artists of later periods. Below, painted on the walls of a cave-temple, is an air spirit, or Apsaras. This dreamy figure, in Indian costume of scarves and heavy jewels, and engulfed by curling clouds, is drawn in the "iron wire" style, in heavy, steady brush lines. This manner of drawing was borne into China from India and was especially favored there in the T'ang era. Facing, are portions of two scrolls. One shows barbarian kings and chiefs, in various northern costumes, offering gifts to the Buddha. The other shows a stocky, heavily robed T'ang woman bathing an infant in a wide, decorated basin.

The bamboo hats are moving!
All the hoes are turning up the soil!
Away with maggots and insects!
For the god of the fields is powerful—let him take them and
  fling them into the blazing fire!

During the Chou period, some three hundred ancient verses were gathered into a group which afterward became treasured as part of the Confucian Classics. These ancient bits of simple poetry then were also given Confucian morals:

Suh-suh *go the rows of the wild geese*
As they rest on the busy mulberry trees.
The king's business must not be performed sloppily
Or we cannot plant our rice and maize—
And how then shall our parents get food?

Slowly, the language of poetry became more personal. "As a frightened bird whose love/Has wandered away from the nest,/I flutter my desolate wings," wrote a Han poet. By T'ang times, the images had become richer; the lines flowing, each one more embroidered than the last, but the plaintive mood is the same and the feeling of connection with the land:

You said you would come, but you did not, and you left me
  with no other trace
Than the moonlight on your tower . . .
Blue burns your candle in its kingfisher-feather lantern . . .
But far beyond my reach is the Enchanted Mountain
And you are on the other side, ten thousand peaks away.

By the mid T'ang era, there were thousands of gifted poets in the Central Kingdom, with a tradition of poetic forms and subjects for their inspiration. Now the singer of chants was no longer the farmer, drawing sustenance from the land he praised in verse, but one who must be fed by the state if he were to have time to write. So it was within the arms of the T'ang bureaucracy that most of these talented men worked. Empress Wu was the first to expand the civil service examination to include a section on writing poetry. After her time, more and more boys with literary talent and ambition left their homes and flocked, every three years, to Ch'ang-an, to prepare for the all-important examinations. If they succeeded, they were heroes to their families, sure at least of a job somewhere in the government service with a little time off to write verse. If they failed, they went back to the village or marketplace, with hope of an artist's life gone forever.

Boarding in hostels and inns in the big city, they crammed the last bits of Confucian doctrine into their skulls. Memory work was the secret to success, for mental agility was favored over original thinking. The Master's way of looking at things must be mastered. Then, hopefully, when the brush was in hand and the sheet of paper before one, answers would flow forth. "Learn all there is to know about bamboos," advised a painter along the same lines. "Study bamboos for ten years. Then when you sit down to draw a bamboo, forget everything you have learned."

A few days after the tests, the results were posted upon the wall of the Board of Rites building. Rejoicing, the winners went off to a great picnic in the Serpentine. Then they were free until their assignments were made. Strolling in the parks, toasting one another with rice wine, these fortunate youths often also made it their business during these weeks to pick out companionable wives who would accompany them wherever they were sent. For soon the wheel of fortune spun and each youth was sent forth to his destiny. Perhaps he would be posted to the imperial libraries themselves, there to write praises of the Emperor and his concubines and heroic memorials of battle. Perhaps, just as likely, he would be sent forth to a rude province where not a congenial person resided. There, in loneliness, he would write verses remembering his student days while, dully, he went through his official routine. Or perhaps he might be sent to a big city—Lo-yang, or Hangchow, or Canton—from which it was a steady progression to the post of provincial governor. Then he would live in pomp and splendor, with mounted guards at his front and back when he ventured out to inspect his domain. Yet at every instant, the poet, like all civil servants, was subject to the whims of the central government; up and down the ladder of merit he might be shifted as the winds in the capital shifted and power-hungry men—whether Taoist priests, or eunuch guards, or in-laws of the Emperor—won the ear of the Son of Heaven.

As if they felt always trapped in this vise of destiny, most of the T'ang poets seem to sing of some vanished freedom. They identify themselves with solitary animals of the landscape—the silver carp brooding in his watery bed; the wild goose winging between mountain peaks; the bluebird windtossed away from his nest.

I am thinking of the White Gate City where I cannot be . . .
I watch a lonely wildgoose in three thousand miles of cloud,

wrote Li Shang-yin.

Now is the time for poetry that remembers summer . . .
For time past escapes from us quicker than a flight of birds,

sang Tu Fu.

The happiness and security of the moment seems always on the brink of fading, and when it goes, life itself is drained of joy:

At night I dreamt I was back in Ch'ang-an,

Po Chü-i confessed.

I saw again the faces of old friends
And in my dreams, under an April sky
They led me by the hand to wander in the spring winds.
Together we came to the village of Peace and Quiet.
Yuan Chen was sitting all alone;
When he saw me coming, a smile came to his face.
He pointed back at the flowers in the western court
Then opened wine in the northern summer house . . .

But then, the dream fades:

I woke up and thought him still at my side . . .
I put out my hand; there was nothing there at all.

It may have been Ming Huang's fascination with the arts that blinded him, as the years went by, to a situation in his empire that boded ill for the future. Painting his own pictures and listening to his poets, he turned most of the prosaic business of the court over to an ambitious minister, who quickly stirred up resentment by trying to streamline the bureaucracy. The allowances made to hangers-on of the court, the old aristocratic families, were cut down. Monks and nuns were turned out of their cloisters and told to earn their keep. The civil service rolls were cut back and some who had enjoyed easy sinecures were thrown on their own resources. Soon, many individuals and families began to board up their houses, pack their goods and move, stealthily, for it was against the law, down to the South, land of new opportunity.

Ming Huang was oblivious to the discontent, absorbed in the delights of his palace. In his Royal Observatory was one of the most brilliant mathematicians of the known world, an Indian with the honored name Gautama Siddhartha, ready to explain a fascinating new concept he was exploring—"zero." The Royal Gardens were heady with lotus and camellias, peonies and exotic palmyras transplanted to Ch'ang-an from India. Troups of foreign dancers and tumblers, puppeteers and performers of shadow plays, were at hand to bring a smile to the imperial features if life became tedious.

Out in the forested hills east of the city was a famous hot springs, where Ming Huang wintered. One mineral pool had been made to look like a universe in miniature, with an island in the center of pure lapis lazuli. On crisp days, a cloud of fragrant steam hung over this pond, and there Ming Huang and his concubines amused themselves in sandalwood and lacquer boats. For his dining table, rare fruits from the southern territories were spilled from barges loaded high, drawing into an enormous staging lake east of Ch'ang-an, which the Emperor had had excavated in 743 to make such commerce easier. But outside these enclaves, China suffered.

From the vermilion gates comes the smell of wine and flesh.
In the road are bones of men who froze to death,

wrote Tu Fu, greatest of Ming Huang's poets, who, like a handful of his fellow-bards, was painfully sensitive to the growing unhappiness in the land:

A hairbreadth divides wealth and utter poverty.
This strange contrast fills me with unending anguish.

Always with Ming Huang, at the hot springs or in the cool rustic retreats of summer, was his favorite, a plump, fish-eyed young beauty named Yang Kuei-fei. Wherever he went, she accompanied him, strumming her lute inlaid with golden phoenixes and strung with silken threads, or playing the childish games with which Ming Huang liked to lighten his days.

For her part, though, Yang Kuei-fei developed a fondness for a barbarian general stationed on the northeastern frontier, An Lu-shan, child of a Turkish mother and a father of the Sogdian tribe of Central Asia. Rising swiftly in the Chinese military hierarchy, An Lu-shan became a frequent visitor to the court in Ch'ang-an, entertaining the Emperor and Yang Kuei-fei with his rowdy jokes and stories. An Lu-shan was grossly fat; his antics shocked the conservative nobles of the court, but to Ming Huang they seemed merely comic.

An Lu-shan had risen into prominence in Hopei Province in northeastern China, which in past times had suffered under several campaigns against Korea. "The officials grind [the people] to the bone and have no pity in their hearts . . ." wrote a historian of this place and time. "The people's flesh smarts under the blows. In their pain, they have no joy in living." The writer foresaw that where suffering exists, revolution may follow. "Now criminals will be sleeping in the dewey grass, hiding out in the hills and marshes. If you pardon them, they will come out. If not, they will become bandits." Bitter toward the imperial armies, Hopei turned treacherously to An Lu-shan when he made up his mind to challenge the court in Ch'ang-an.

It is hard to know just how events proceeded, for the chronicles of the time are filled, as always, with justifications after the fact, laying the whole blame for the crippling of T'ang power on An Lu-shan. "His mother was a Turkish magician," went the tale. "She had no son and prayed to Ya-lo-shan. The god answered and he was born. On that night, a red light shone by his side; all the wild animals howled. A star of evil magic fell on the tent . . . When he grew up, he was a vicious thief, cruel, full of wiles." But there are conflicting reports too, to the effect that An Lu-shan was brave and, for a time, loyal to his Emperor. However, it is certain that he took advantage of a series of natural disasters—famine, rainstorms which rotted the imperial stockpiles of grain, a conflagration which destroyed Ch'ang-an's principal arsenal—to gather together and inflame an army of hardened, rebellious soldiers.

In 755, An Lu-shan and his army marched southward, along an open route toward the eastern capital Lo-yang, which they took without difficulty. Next he marched on Ch'ang-an, broke through the eastern mountain pass which guarded the city, and captured it. Apparently, the teeth of the Central Kingdom had decayed during Ming Huang's pacifistic reign. For too long there had been "peace, in the middle plain. The Emperor had the spear and arrow points melted down . . . Men grew to old age without hearing the sound of war." At the end, tragically, when An Lu-shan was at the gates, "their knees shook and they were incapable of carrying arms . . . After this, rebels took advantage of the situation to revolt." The city fell into chaos and rival warlords sprang up in An Lu-shan's wake to dispute the territories he had ravaged.

Ming Huang and his court had to flee for their lives. They escaped toward the west, but when the train grew weary and stopped at a post station to rest, Ming Huang's guards mutinied. They refused to accompany him farther unless he turned over to them the person they held responsible for the catastrophe. Thus Yang Kuei-fei was handed over to the soldiers, who took her into the garden and hanged her from the branch of a tree.

The tale of Ming Huang's flight from Ch'ang-an and the death of his beloved Yang Kuei-fei was not forgotten in China, even when uneasy peace had been restored. Some fifty years after the event, one of China's greatest poets, Po Chu-i, wrote a long series of verses describing Yang's arrival at court and her training in the imperial manners:

> *. . . They bathed her in the Flower-pure Pool . . .*
> *The cloud of her hair, petal of her cheek, gold ripples of her crown*
>   *when she moved,*
> *Were sheltered on spring evenings by warm hibiscus curtains.*

For generations, Chinese families had prayed for the birth of boys, to work the fields and bring honor to their ancestors in the civil examinations. But now, since Yang had become so famous,

> *She brought to every father, every mother through the empire*
> *Happiness when a girl was born instead of a boy.*

But then disaster struck.

> *War drums, booming from Yüyang, shocked the whole earth . . .*

The Emperor and his court fled for their lives:

> *The Forbidden City, the nine-tiered palace, loomed in the dust*
> *From thousands of horses and chariots headed southwest . . .*

And Yang met her death at the hands of the palace guards:

> *Flowery hairpins fell to the ground. No one picked them up . . .*
> *The Emperor could not save her. He could only cover his face.*

Po Chü-i was not the only poet to be deeply moved by the historical events which had shaken his country. Others, who lived during the years of An Lu-shan's rebellion, recorded the tragedy at first hand. Eleven years before the march on Ch'ang-an, the poet Li Po had been visiting in Hopei province and there seen evidence of preparation for war. Still, as a youth he had firmly made up his mind to "keep aloof from the world," so he tried to lose himself in courtly pleasures and in wine and music.

> *From a pot of wine among the flowers*
> *I drank alone . . .*
> *I sang. The moon encouraged me.*
> *I danced. My shadow tumbled after . . .*
> *And then I was drunk, and we lost one another . . .*
> *I watch the long road of the River of Stars.*

He spent some time as a hermit, studying with a Buddhist monk until he reached the level of ecstasy called "windwheel," letting his mind spin like a top through space.

He climbed the peaks of east China, riding on a white deer and meeting fairies who gave him "liquid mist" to release him from the earth.

> *Oh, but it is high and very dangerous!*
> *Such traveling is harder than scaling the blue sky . . .*
> *Panting, we brush Orion and pass the Well Star.*
> *Even to hear of it turns the cheek pale,*
> *With the highest crag barely a foot below heaven . . .*

He fled again to the mountains with a band of drinking companions and some Taoist monks and nuns. He dabbled in magic with his friends, "Rise in the Air" and "Seeker of Truth."

But when he looked across the valley, he saw young soldiers torn from their families marching through the passes to the battle line drawn up in southern Honan against An Lu-shan.

> *An old mother is parting from her son.*
> *She cries to heaven, standing in the wild scrub . . .*

He hated war, and in this Li Po was no different from the Confucian masters. "Our body and hair and skin are all derived from our parents," states the Confucian Book of Filial Piety. "Therefore we have no right to injure any of them in the least. This is the first duty of a child."

And yet, since the dawn of Chinese civilization, there had been enemies waiting to plunge the land into chaos, and beyond the Wall, the Tartar nomads:

The king's armies have grown old and gray
Fighting ten thousand leagues away from home.
The Huns have no trade but battle and carnage
They have no fields or ploughlands
But only wastes where white bones lie among yellow sands.
There the House of Ch'in built the Great Wall to keep away the Tartars.
There, in turn, the House of Han lit beacons of war.
The beacons are always alight, fighting and marching never stop.
Men die in the field, slashing sword to sword.
The horses of the conquered neigh piteously . . .

The poet Tu Fu also witnessed the disastrous events: between 756 and 757 he was trapped in occupied Ch'ang-an. There he saw streets once thronging with people now dark and vacant. The splendid houses on the banks of the Serpentine lake, whose owners had fled to the western province of Szechwan, were shuttered. Wherever he turned, despair held the land in its grip.

I hear women in the distance wailing after the battle;
. . . Sleeping-Dragon, Plunging-Horse, are no generals now;
they are dust—
Hush for a moment, O tumult of the world!

When at last Tu Fu regained his own home after many months, he found tragedy had struck his family: "When I entered the gate, I heard a sound of weeping. My little son had died for want of food."

The writings of these poets, commemorating the great events of their time or simply describing the splendor and darkness of it were written in graceful calligraphy or printed from wood blocks onto pieces of paper or silk. These were passed from hand to hand between friends, or even pasted onto the walls of public buildings for multitudes to enjoy. One poetry-lover of the T'ang period even had Po Chü-i's verses tattooed all over his body!

Eventually, in the Sung Dynasty, moveable type was invented in China, still centuries before Gutenberg had the same idea in the West. Then books of poems were turned out in great number, and the Imperial Libraries rapidly added to their collections. The greatest of these libraries belonged to the eighteenth-century Emperor Ch'ien Lung, of the Ch'ing Dynasty. He possessed works by over two thousand T'ang poets alone. But before him, the T'ang emperors themselves, beginning with T'ai Tsung, amassed a library of over 200,000 scrolls. These were divided into four sections—classics, histories, philosophies, and collections—and distinguished by different colored ties, tabs and rollers. A scroll of Li Po's poems in Ming Huang's library, for example, would turn upon a green roller and be fastened with white tabs and a vermilion tie. A scroll of Confucian maxims would have a white roller, red tabs and a yellow tie. When Ming Huang inherited the T'ang library, he set his scholars to work in academies in both Ch'ang-an and Lo-yang, copying the ancient scrolls and making new ones. In these efforts, he was following the example of his ancestors, for even the Han emperors possessed a magnificent library at the Cloud Terrace in Lo-yang.

But the years brought desolation. As the Han Cloud Terrace and its treasures had gone up in smoke, so T'ai Tsung's great library was decimated in its time, beginning with the armies of An Lu-shan. By the eleventh century, over half of the T'ang books had vanished forever, together with the Palace of Great Brightness itself.

Chapter IX The End of Brightness

. . . happiness had ended at the Court of the Bright Sun.
(PO CHÜ-I)

Once he had swept the north of China. An Lu-shan's ambitions were satisfied; he had neither the desire nor the genius to expand his holdings nor to rule what he had conquered. He occupied Ch'ang-an for a few months until he was murdered by a Chinese youth he had adopted. The imperial family was allowed to return to the Palace City, but Ming Huang, desolate without his Yang Kuei-fei, seemed broken in body and spirit. His Empire had been reduced to fragments. Where the rebels had fought, feudal warlords had sprung up either to oppose or join them. When peace was restored, these new rebels grimly held onto their domains, and without an Imperial Guard commanded from a central post, China's cities now lay open to invasion. In 763, an army of Tibetans forged into Ch'ang-an, burning and destroying what An Lu-shan had left. Eventually they were repelled, but the great city had suffered too much ever to regain its brilliant position. Between 755, when Ming Huang stepped down, until 907, when the T'ang Dynasty finally expired, thirteen emperors succeeded one another, some weak and short-lived, others vigorous, but none who could recreate the days of the past.

And yet, as in the late days of Rome's ascendancy over the Mediterranean world, Ch'ang-an continued to receive tribute from the lands bordering on the southern seas, and a class of ever-richer bureaucrats, often siphoning off gold and other booty from their appointed provinces, enjoyed what they owned as if their world would last forever. In 815, for instance, chronicles announce the arrival in Canton of a shipment of "exotic aromatics" from Java: incense, resins, rare woods, patchouli and other products destined for the Buddhist temples and aristocratic homes of Ch'ang-an. Slaves and royal visitors fram afar sailed to the Central Kingdom. Once, an embassy from a mysterious southern "Country of Female Peoples" came to bow before the Dragon Throne. Their sleek bodies were adorned with beads; piled high, their black tresses were crowned with golden hats. Struck by the mystery of these people who spoke a foreign tongue yet bore themselves with dignity, the residents of Ch'ang-an named them the "Bodhisattva People," or saints of Buddha. Another time, a famous "Black-eyebrow Maiden" was sent to Ch'ang-an to entertain the imperial family. Such was her skill that she could embroider all seven scrolls of one Buddhist sutra, or holy story, onto one foot of Chinese silk. She lived in luxury at the Palace for a number of years and then, according to legend, returned to the land from which she had been abducted, died, and thereafter was seen floating on a purple cloud over her beloved, warm-water seas.

Efforts were made by many to shore up the old Empire. In 819, an official, Han Yü, was sent to a post in the distant south, where, for some time, the coastal villages had been plagued by crocodiles. Bravely, Han Yü went out and stood upon the beach. Lifting his voice in ceremonial style, he delivered a thunderous speech to the beasts, explaining that in earlier times when the Empire was strong, they had never dared threaten the people. Now, he proclaimed, Chinese forces once again controlled the South. Either the whole tribe of crocodiles must forthwith depart, or he would order his men to shoot poisoned arrows into the water.

Other men of the government had more practical advice to give the Emperor. Some laid the blame for the disintegration of the Dynasty on Ming Huang. Others felt strongly that it was the fault of the Buddhist hierarchy, which continued to drain off money from the treasury into their temples and monasteries. These moreover sapped the energy of the land by preaching that work was useless and the world only a passing dream. In 819, a spokesman for this point of view addressed the Emperor, saying that Buddhism was "one of the practices of barbarian peoples." No worse insult could be delivered; the so-called barbarians were still, as always, considered a race beneath the Chinese, hardly human, with no trait or idea worthy enough to be adopted by the Central Kingdom. The advisor, Han Yü, delivered a further insult: "Buddha himself was a barbarian. His language differed from the Chinese. His clothes were of a different cut.

"Suppose," he went on, "Buddha were living today. You might well give him a feast, and a gift. But then you would take him to the border so he would not mislead the people."

As tribes around the Central Kingdom waxed more powerful on their own, the traditional indulgence of the Chinese toward foreigners, which was partly based on military superiority over them, began to erode. For centuries, the Uighurs, who, in their tall hats and heavy cloaks, had thronged Ch'ang-an as dealers of the best horse flesh, had been allowed to come and go as they wished. But as China's economy weakened, and her generals clamored for more cavalry to resist invasion, the Uighurs became arrogant. The price of a good mount rose to forty bolts of Chinese silk. In one deal, China agreed to pay a million bolts of taffeta in exchange for the warhorses her experts demanded. In 799, an edict was published which compelled the Uighurs to appear in the streets of Ch'ang-an only in full native costume so they could be easily picked out of the crowd by observers from the imperial court. Moreover, they were forbidden henceforth to marry Chinese women and to settle down in the Central Kingdom. In 843, the Persian Manicheans too were the victims of a restrictive edict. The next year, persecutions began against the Buddhists.

Withdrawn, meditating and praying, in their self-sufficient monasteries, the Buddhists apparently did little to protect themselves or to plead their cause before the Emperor. Soon, the imperial guards were authorized to break into the temples and monasteries, to collect the holy treasures, to burn those which seemed useless and to melt down the bronze and gold images. At the end, over 40,000 monasteries were shut down and many of them razed. Some 400,000 monks and nuns were turned out and ordered to marry and take up an active, socially responsible life. Eventually, the Nestorian and Zoroastrian temples too came under attack and their metal statues were melted down for farm implements, weapons or new money. Thus, treasures which had survived the sacking of Ch'ang-an by An Lu-shan and the Tibetans now met their fate.

At the end of the ninth century, new disasters befell the land. An army posted in the far South, land of jungles and crocodiles, rebelled against the conditions in their camps, and joining under the leadership of a rebel named Huang Ch'ao, marched down to the port of Canton. Here, they massacred perhaps 120,000 foreign merchants and traders—Arabs, Nestorians, Persians, Indonesians. Then the disorganized troops slashed down the precious Cantonese mulberry groves, heart of her silk manufacture. From these attacks, Canton never recovered.

In 881, Huang Ch'ao's rebels turned north toward Ch'ang-an itself. Once more, the great city was laid waste. Thereafter, independent warlords squabbled over the ruins.

Eventually, the strongest of these overcame his rivals. The last inhabitants of the city were exterminated. The walls and buildings were knocked down. The once rubbed and polished, carved and painted beams that had held aloft the winged roofs of the Palace of Great Brightness were heaped into boats and floated downstream for a new settlement.

By this time, the T'ang Empire hardly existed in any case. A century before, Tun-huang had been taken by the Tibetans. After 821, the unprotected northern silkroutes were held by shifting tribes—the Uighurs, their enemies, the Kirghiz and others. There too, the Turks were again massing into well-organized fighting bands.

According to the chronicles, written after the fact as always, it was time again for the Mandate of Heaven to slip out of the grasp of men who had failed to be worthy of its burden.

Among the famous visitors to China during this late phase of the T'ang Dynasty was a Japanese monk named Ennin. Like old Hsüan-tsang who went the westward path to India to learn the teachings of Buddha, Ennin also traveled in the direction of the setting sun to find what he considered to be the truth. In 834, he set out across the Yellow Sea and soon came to a spill of water from the mighty Yangtze, "whitish water the color of yellow mud . . . flowing from the Great River of Yang-Chou."

Slowly Ennin proceeded upstream and overland, visiting monasteries and taking notes on the commonplace and wonderful things he saw. "It was very hot," he wrote one day, still in the humid south. "At two P.M. it thundered . . . mosquitoes large as flies . . ."

"All night," he remembered, "drums were beaten . . . watchmen who, when night comes, beat drums to guard government property."

One day thirteen monks paid him a visit. They introduced themselves and announced, "Quite idly and without attachments, like clouds floating about the landscape, we came down from Wu Feng and wandered to Ch'u Su . . . happy to pay you our respects."

The governor of a certain district next called on Ennin. He arrived at the head of a column of two hundred foot soldiers dressed in blue-gray. Behind, in ranks, were forty military police and eighty riders. Ennin gave his guest two strings of crystal beads, six silver razors, twenty bamboo brushes and three conch shells. The governor reciprocated with two lengths of fine white China silk and three of damask.

One New Year's Eve, Ennin watched the people burning paper money and stacks of bamboo and shouting—as he said—"Banzai!" "Lamps without number" were hung from the trees and rafters on the night of the full moon. Then when spring came, he saw children buying little clay figurines of orioles, painted orange and black, harbingers of the sweet breezes of summer. And when summer followed, flowers so fragrant and beautiful grew in the gardens—crocus and lilies, peonies and lotus—they seemed "not of the world of men."

In 840, Ennin arrived in the capital. There, he became a sharp observer of the anti-Buddhist campaign. At first, he noted, the program seemed to be based on a quite reasonable wish to strengthen the economy and return the enormous class of cloistered monks to the fields and shops. But slowly, the attacks became more virulent. Finally word came to Ennin that the Emperor had decided to slaughter all the Buddhist clerics in Ch'ang-an. So he and a number of compatriots decided to go home. "We packed books, scriptures, magic diagrams into four baskets," he wrote. "We bought three donkeys," and off they went.

You were destined to find the source,

wrote a T'ang Dynasty poet, Ch'ien Ch'i, of a Japanese Buddhist priest who, like Ennin, had come to the Central Kingdom to learn the true teachings of Buddha and was now homeward bound:

Now, tracing your way as in a dream
You fade from the world in your fragile boat . . .
Fishes and dragons follow your chanting,
And the eye still watches, beyond the horizon,
The light of your single lantern.

So Ennin, and many other foreigners, once welcome in the Central Kingdom, took their leave. After the T'ang Dynasty disappeared, Japan, like China, was to draw into herself and cast off foreign influences. Thereafter, confined in an insular world, the Japanese threw themselves into the creation of works of art with a distinctly national character: golden screens painted with cranes and chrysanthemums, woodblock prints of women in gorgeous kimonos, landscape paintings more brittle than Chinese models, and stunning works in lacquer and ceramic. These later works of Japanese artisans caught the eye of Westerners in the nineteenth century. But by that time, most of the works of T'ang, from which these originally had evolved, had long been lost to sight on the mainland, sunk like the little pilgrim's boat into the realm of "fishes and dragons," of fantasy and garbled memory.

Chapter X Sung and Yüan

For a half-century after the final dismemberment of the T'ang Empire, China lay in ruins. Five separate regimes rose and collapsed. At last, one military officer, with the help of his generals, managed to lift himself to a position of supreme power. Once enthroned, the new emperor, Chao K'uang-yin, took stock and came to an important conclusion: if his generals were allowed to retain their posts, each one would, in time, hunger for power of his own. Inevitably, China would be driven back into the cycle of civil war.

Shortly after he assumed his title, therefore, Chao K'uang-yin invited the generals to a banquet. After they had eaten and drunk and been soothed by the music of lutes and ocarinas playing the ancient tunes they loved, he opened the conversation.

"I do not sleep peacefully at night," he said.

"Why not?" inquired the generals, no doubt surprised at this confession.

"It is obvious," replied the Emperor. "Is there any one of you who does not secretly wish he were on my throne?"

The generals at once raised their voices protesting that such a thing was impossible, but the Emperor continued, "The life of man is short. Happiness is in enjoying life and having some wealth, and leaving some of that wealth to one's descendants." Then he made a proposal. "If you, my officers, will all give up your army posts and authority, and retire to the provinces, I will make sure you have a beautiful house there, and the best land on which to dwell. There you can pass the rest of your lives without any peril or uncertainty. And, to prove that I will always consider you close to my heart, I will arrange marriages between my family and all of yours."

According to historians, the generals accepted the offer at once. The very next morning, each submitted his resignation. Then each retired into the mountains and lived out his life in prosperity and tranquility. It was a plan of great foresight, but principally it fit the mood of the times. At this moment in history, the Chinese were exhausted with the wars which had torn their land and hungered for inner peace and security.

The peace which marked the three-hundred-year long Sung Dynasty was bought, however, at a heavy price—one which irrevocably set China upon a path apart from the rest of the world. At the north, slowly but surely, the gateways through which a flood of international ideas and products had entered during the T'ang Dynasty were swinging shut. In the northeast, Khitan tribes were settling into territory traditionally under Chinese control. The Sung emperors, not wishing to engage in border warfare, allowed them to do so, even paying tribute to them to keep the peace. The Khitans themselves settled into Chinese ways, but other hordes not so pacific were gathering at their rear.

At the northwest too, a barbarian people, the Hsi Hsia, held the marches. No more caravans plied the great silk routes, and the Buddhist cave temples along the way lay in abandon, their stone and stucco Buddhas in a sleep from which they would not awaken until the arrival of Aurel Stein and other explorers of the twentieth century.

As the political borders closed and China's preoccupations turned inward, the character of her arts and philosophy changed. Where the T'ang had been robust and militaristic, flush with curiosity about foreign arts and foreign gods, the Sung closed their eyes to these influences, and though

Buddhist temples continued to be served in the cities, began to absorb themselves in the old Confucian and Taoist ideas. No more rugged stone sculptures were made, nor even the hardy little grave figures that enlivened T'ang tombs. If a figure of Kuan-yin, goddess of mercy, was required now, she would be carved out of wood, graceful and tender, lifting her soft hand in a gesture of peaceful benediction.

Concern for the quality of life of the people, too, was a new preoccupation. The first printed books, made from wood blocks, had appeared in the ninth century, but now books printed from moveable type came onto the market, and bookshops sprang up in the principal cities. Soon the average man would be able to stock a small library with adventure tales, plays, and short stories.

A sense of social responsibility began to be felt as well. One imperial minister, Wang An-shih, tried to work out a series of measures to help China's peasants. He cut the imperial budget by forty percent and raised all the civil salaries. He set up banks to arrange for loans to the peasants so they would not be forced into debt to village money-lenders. As others had done before him, he organized the peasants into small groups, which had responsibility for keeping peace and stamping out banditry in each sector. Wang An-shih was not unconscious, either, of the danger threatening China from the north, and he tried to persuade her people to breed horses so a strong cavalry would be available in case of attack. But in the end, Wang An-shih's ideas proved to be too advanced for his time. After some months, he was retired out of government service and his measures were taken off the books.

It was, perhaps, the Sung artists who best expressed their times. In the new capital city of Kaifeng, and in the valleys and spiny mountains around it, a school of landscape painters appeared who took ideas born in the T'ang and made of them one of the supreme art forms of the world. These artists, like those of the T'ang before them, often painted on a long, horizontally rolled-up scroll. Bit by bit, one could turn the scroll in both hands, uncovering only a small section at a time, as if one were looking at a moving picture. Most of the artists now concentrated on landscapes, creating miniature worlds in which thrusting rocks, twisting pines, lonely hermits, and peaceful lakes took on the same, changing fascination as a panoply of living individuals. Though each of these paintings may at first look much like all the others, there were subtle differences between them, and cliques of artists

By the Sung period, the spirit of Chinese art had mellowed. Here Kuan-yin, goddess of mercy, sits in deep, languid meditation on her island in the southern seas.

developed, each working in ways they felt best expressed the "Tao" in the landscape. Artists of one school, for instance, liked the craggy, jagged mountain scenes of the North, while many others preferred the soft, misty, melancholy hills and rain-soaked valleys of the southern landscape. Still others, harking back to the iron-wire conventions of the T'ang and earlier periods, specialized in jewel-like studies of birds or flowers—a branch of white jasmine, or a goldfinch upon a twig of peachblossoms. One great master was Ma Yuan, called "one-corner Ma" because he invented a chopped-off sort of picture with only a few lines or smudges of soft, blurred ink set against a gulf of empty space. Another was Hsia Kuei, whose major work captured the Yangtze River from its beginnings in the western hills, down through plunging gorges and out into the tranquil flatlands of the rice country. Probably Hsia Kuei also meant to teach, by this great composition, that man's life and the life of the empire, too, must pass through struggle and confusion until it achieves at last the tranquil waters of Tao.

A late emperor of the Northern Sung, Hui Tsung, was a painter himself, as many Sung aristocrats were. He particularly loved the paintings of the T'ang Dynasty and spent much of his time copying those precious few which had survived. But perhaps because he was so absorbed in his art, he ignored the frontier of his empire, where a new Tartar people, the Kin, were gradually usurping grounds which, for two hundred years, the Khitans had occupied with permission of the Chinese. Eventually, the Khitans fled west to Turkestan, where, before long, adventurous travelers from Europe would hear about them in a name garbled in translation—Cathayans. And so, in their early ignorance, they would call northern China by the name "Cathay."

In 1126, Emperor Hui Tsung was forced by the Kin to give up at once his brushes and his throne. He was taken prisoner and died roaming with his captors on the northern steppes, far from the finches and flowering bamboo of his painting studio. The remnants of the Sung court fled south and set up a new capital at Hangchow. There, for another century and a half, the Sungs continued to rule a shrunken empire, split off from the mountains, plains and rivers where civilization had flowered in the times of Han and T'ang. And there, like the Yangtze in its long push to the sea, Chinese civilization continued to unroll.

In the southern courts and academies, a number of important schools of philosophers now developed, arguing among themselves about various

The greatest invention of Sung artists, and perhaps one of the greatest inventions of world art, was the horizontal landscape scroll. Painted with ink and pale washes on a long strip of silk, the scene (left; details above) unrolls from right to left and is meant to be read as a long, poetic "moving picture." The connoisseur of Chinese art would slowly turn this work on its ivory rollers, letting his eyes follow the rise of mountains, the spread of water, the feathery touches of trees. Doing so, one comes upon tiny men and women. They push off from land in a little boat. Across empty water, one finds again the dwellings of men, a lonely fisherman, cascading waterfalls, and little travelers on burrows wending their way along a rocky path. At last, the mountains become less rugged, a mist seems to settle in, the painter's hand grows less precise, and this scroll, "Streams and Mountains without End," closes on an abstract note.

points in Confucian doctrine. They debated whether the nature of man is good or evil, or whether, like water churning in a rocky gorge, man's character is shaped by his life's experience, becoming forceful and determined or senselessly chaotic. These men tried to understand how the element of "Li," that "right principle" of which Confucius had spoken, exhibits itself through the universe, as a crystal grows along certain lines, a tree unfolds from an acorn, and men, if they try, gradually come closer to the right way of behaving. Sometimes, too, they argued about whether the policy of pacifism which their emperors had adopted was more akin to the teachings of Confucius, or whether they should have more aggressively defended their nation against the invaders from the north. And it is quite likely true that, as some said, it was because of their deliberate ignorance of the movements of barbarian peoples there, that China now became vulnerable to the most savage host of warriors the world had ever seen.

Messages from the Kin, arriving in the southern capital, sounded the alarm. At the northern gates were the Mongol hordes, under the leadership of Genghis Khan. The Kin too were in their path. "We are the lips," the Kin cried out to their one-time foes, now their only hope for help, "and you are the teeth. If the lips are gone, the teeth will feel the cold." But the Sung emperors ignored the calls. Soon the enemy was pouring through the Jade Gate. Kin and Chinese peasants alike frantically crowded into the cities, hoping for protection behind the earthen walls, but Genghis would not be stopped. If a city offered a single moment's defense, if a single arrow was let fly, the city would be razed and every man, woman, and child slaughtered. Then, Genghis boasted, twelve horsemen could ride abreast where the walls had once stood. "The greatest joy," he is reported to have said, "is to conquer one's enemies, to pursue them, to seize their property, to see their families in tears . . ."

In 1258, the Mongols had totally destroyed the magnificent western Asian city of Baghdad. Then, inch by inch, the once irrigated and farmed plains of Central Asia were reduced to sand drifts from which they have never recovered. Eventually, Hangchow itself, in the southeast of China, fell. The last Sung Emperor was only a child. He was trapped on a ship in the China Sea, and his prime minister, rather than give up the last flower of the Dynasty, took the boy in his arms and leapt into the waves.

In 1260, Genghis' grandson, Kublai Khan, inherited the Mongol standard. Abandoning the old Mongol capital in the north, he set up a new center

By the Sung period, and even more as the centuries unrolled in China, artists began to specialize in one or another kind of painting, which each would then try to carry to its most perfect pitch. Some artists concentrated on landscape scrolls, developing their mastery of brushwork until they could depict the myriad forms of leaves and rocks with just a flick of the brush. Others concentrated on portraits, or pictures of birds and flowers. The motive always, according to Taoist theory, was to catch the "life breath" of a particular scene or image, rather than to show it in its natural background, perspective and proportion.

near the modern city of Peking, proclaimed himself the inheritor of Heaven's Mandate and, in 1271, opened a new dynasty, named the Yüan. Meanwhile, parts of the enormous Mongol empire had broken off to be ruled by other members of his family, all under the remote kingship of Kublai. Persia, for example, was now possessed by his brother, Hulagu, and into the artistic workshops of the Near East, Chinese influences began to filter: dragons and flying birds, clouds and trees, drawn in fluttery brush strokes within the format of the jewel-like manuscript pages which Persian artists had long been turning out. As Kublai's influence stretched almost to the gates of Europe, for the first time in centuries peace embraced this vast arc of the world. An Italian merchant who was preparing a guidebook for overland travelers to China wrote, "The road you travel from Tana [a port on the Black Sea] to Cathay is perfectly safe by day or by night."

Yet for the native Chinese, the Yüan Dynasty was a period of bitterness. Institutions on which the harmonious working of the Chinese government depended were shaken. The peasants suffered under crushing taxes; the courts of law degenerated; the mandarins of the court were forced to accept strict conventions about the language they could speak and even the colors of gown they could wear. With even more reason than before, sensitive men now withdrew into Taoist meditation and their landscape painting in remote mountain hideaways where the guards of the Mongol court could not find them.

At many periods from this point onward, the energies of the Chinese were directed inward, with a negligence toward the rest of the world which some scholars feel is still reflected in her political posture today. And yet, paradoxically, from then on, the rest of the world was never again to let China alone. The Sung had come into power during the tenth century, Europe's darkest phase. But slowly, as the year one thousand came and passed, Europe shook off her backwardness and energetically began to push outward. Soon the Romanesque and then Gothic civilizations had their flowering in Italy and France, and the products of Cathay were hungrily coveted by these traders, Popes, and noblemen for their churches and castles. The Son of Heaven, drawing his robes close about him and standing upon the wreckage of cities of which even he had lost the memory, permitted his merchants, for whom he had little respect, to engage in trade with these new barbarians, while he and his court of Confucian mandarins maintained a posture of forbidding exclusiveness.

Epilogue

When Aurel Stein traveled through Chinese Turkestan, he was pained to see peasant women hobbling between the furrows of their fields on bound feet. Yet we know this convention, which crippled peasant women and also their richer sisters who were carried about in palanquins, stemmed from the love men of the late T'ang and Sung dynasties felt for dancers with feet slim as "jade bamboo shoots." In a world which, century by century, grew more open and interdependent, China's suspicious attitude toward regions outside the Central Kingdom, which was justified when their enemies ranged the marshes, became just as tight a yoke upon her society as those cloth rags upon her women's feet.

By the twentieth century, it was apparent that Chinese society had failed to keep pace with the West or to bring to fulfillment the cosmopolitan view which had emerged during epochs like the T'ang. For, from the Yüan Dynasty until the fall of the Manchu in 1912, China, like a sea anemone in changing tides, had opened and closed her mind to the West almost whimsically, according to the taste of each emperor and his intuition of what foreigners had in mind.

In the thirteenth century, Marco Polo, for example, came to the Dragon Throne out of curiosity, deferential and willing to serve, and thus spent seventeen years working for Kublai Khan. He visited Kanbaluc, now Peking, and the Khan's summer retreat in the hills north of Peking. There, in the palace called Shandu, he saw "halls and chambers all gilt . . . with rich and beautiful meadows where deer are pastured." He visited the "royal pavilion on a colonnade of pillars, gilt and varnished. Round each pillar a dragon entwines its tail." Apparently the old T'ang style of architecture had been somewhat transformed by Mongolian tastes, for Polo reported that "the building is supported on every side like a tent by more than two hundred strong silken cords." Nor had the ancient Chinese form of nature worship held out against the influence of nomad customs. Once a year, at an August festival, the Khan scattered milk from his sacred milk-white horses as a libation to the gods.

Marco Polo visited Hangchow, one of the most beautiful cities in the world at this time, built across a scattering of islands, so that the tranquil blue of lagoons was broken by the diminutive arching of thousands of stone bridges and the gilded, stacked-up roofs of pagodas. Between Hangchow and other cities, Polo traveled without anxiety, along broad roads and between post houses where his horses could be rested. Along these roads mail passed swiftly and safely, and, "in the fruit season, what is gathered in the morning at Kanbaluc is conveyed to the Grand Khan at Shandu by the evening of the following day."

China was then in the hands of a ruler who was actively curious about the rest of the world. Many ideas found shelter within Kublai Khan's court, and though he did not feel constrained to accept them for his own, he was willing to be convinced otherwise. Though the Mongols practiced a Buddhism tinged with occult Tibetan ideas, he listened when Marco Polo pleaded the cause of Christianity. "Wherefore should I become a Christian?" he inquired. Other lands had holy men who could perform miracles, fill empty cups with wine or make it rain. "What extraordinary powers have been displayed by the ministers of Christianity?" he asked again, and invited Marco Polo's Pope to send him some miracle-working priests to convince him.

But the Pope did not think it worthwhile to convert Cathay, and the opportunity was not soon to be presented again. Within a century, the disintegrating Yüan Empire was wrested away from the Mongols by a former Chinese Buddhist monk turned bandit and rebel. Having no family fief after which to name his reign, he called it the Ming, or "Brilliant" Dynasty. The Ming emperors were orthodox Confucians, absorbed with the past. Trade westward was not encouraged, and it gradually shriveled. After Marco Polo, it was three centuries before men came again by the overland route to the Dragon Throne.

But the hunger for trade and exploration that Westerners were beginning to feel could not be stopped. In 1453, Byzantium fell to the Turks. Now there was no possibility of trade across the deserts of the Near East. Yet men were impelled to find a way to the coffers of Cathay. Maps and charts were now turned out with sufficient accuracy so that ships could hope to sail and return, and printed books supplied encouraging reports of earlier adventurers. In 1498, Vasco da Gama pushed his boat, for all he knew, into the very mouth of the Leviathan, and ended up at the Indian port of Calicut. He came home with a cargo of Malaya pepper, and thereafter his king, Manuel I of Portugal, called himself "Lord of the Conquest, Navigation and Commerce of India, Ethiopia, Arabia and Persia." Eighteen years later, the first Portuguese ship touched at Canton.

Unfortunately, this early wave of seagoing Westerners consisted of men in the spirit of Pizzarro and Cortez, who destroyed the Indian civilizations of Central America for the gold that darkly shines in Spanish and Portuguese cathedrals even today. Brutally, they attacked unguarded Chinese boats and plundered ports which were unused to attack by sea. The result was that soon foreign traders were forbidden to travel outside certain sections of the harbor cities. Now and then, an ambassador bearing the highest references from his state might be allowed, strictly chaperoned and instructed at every step in the arcane ritual, to present "tribute" to the emperor and receive in return the haughty nod of the Son of Heaven. But even this intercourse was discouraged. In 1656, Emperor Shun Chih summed up the attitude in a mandate to the ambassador from the Netherlands, which had followed Spain and Portugal in the next century as principal trader and colonizer in the East: "When we think of the danger of storm and shipwreck that besets the passage hither," said Shun Chih, "we are too solicitous of the Dutch people to do more than permit them to send ships to China once in eight years."

Yet there had, even if rarely, been Westerners who traveled with goals other than material ones. A number of these in the seventeenth century were Jesuits, but less zealous than their brothers then promoting the Inquisition in Spain. One in particular, Matteo Ricci, made a place for himself at the imperial court, instructing the mandarins in astronomy and medicine, while learning the Chinese language and trying to master the principles of Chinese philosophy. Ricci spent nine years in Peking and apparently at the end was loved for his gentle humanity as well as his "curly beard, blue eyes and voice like a great bell." But he had faced the traditional hostility when he arrived. "The images and paintings of the Lord of Heaven and of a virgin which Li Ma-tou [Ricci] offers as tribute are not of great value," the Board of Rites had announced when he appeared. "He offers a purse in which he says there are the bones of immortals, as if the immortals, when they ascend to heaven, did not take their bones with them . . . We advise therefore . . . that he should be sent back to his own country." It was apparently, however, the seriousness with which Ricci treated ideas which the Chinese also took seriously that opened the doors. Benedict de Goes, whose grave Aurel Stein visited near the Great Wall, was another Jesuit, a contemporary of Ricci, whose affection for Cathay had brought him close to its forbidden areas.

It was, however, Europe of the eighteenth century that most amorously embraced China. Big companies founded in the seventeenth century, the Dutch and British East India Companies, and the Companie de Chine, were now unloading great shipments of Chinese art and merchandise at Amsterdam and other ports. The great arts of the T'ang and Sung had by now degenerated: monumental sculpture was made no more and painting was pursued as a scholar's obsession. The new arts, well suited for export, were small and decorative, particularly porcelains.

Since the T'ang Dynasty, Chinese porcelain-makers had been experimenting with clays and glazes and gradually refining their techniques at the imperial pottery works of Ching-tê-chen, where night and day, flames and black smoke from thousands of furnaces colored the sky. Vessels were turned out for the most part in a few shapes handed down from the days of Shang, but now with glazes and enamel finishes of dazzling variety. There

A

B

C

Among the greatest arts invented and then
perfected in China were ceramic vessels. In
T'ang times, these often owed their rugged
shape with animal-headed handles, to metal-
workers of the Near East (top). But by Sung
and Ming eras, the shapes were refined to a
point of great simplicity, while the glazes became ever more elaborate, and surfaces were
adorned with brilliant colors and flowing patterns.

were "raven's wing purple," and "snakeskin green." There were "sang de boeuf," a resonant dark red, and "clair de lune," an intangible blue, and vases whose background color—green, rose, black or yellow—was enlivened with lyrical entwining plum and apple boughs, and birds and butterflies hovering in space. The most precious Chinese vases, often in an earthy but ethereal gray-green called "celadon," were sometimes set by western gold-smiths into bronze wrappings as one might set off a jewel. Toward the end of the eighteenth century, a combination blue and white "china" became so popular with western housekeepers that factories were set up in Holland to imitate it more cheaply.

Love of things Chinese absorbed all Europe. Rococo castles were given salons whose walls sparkled with inlaid placques of Chinese porcelain. In England, Thomas Chippendale designed furniture with sleepy mandarins nodding their heads beneath parasols and pagodas. At the French court, the king, in robes of embroidered silk, guided the plow through the first furrow in a Chinese New Year's festival for the amuse-ment of Madame Pompadour. Even gardens of the time were designed in Chinese style as a contrast to the geometric formality of the French or Italian garden. So much did these tangled, "poetic" gardens delight city planners of the West that, a century later, Central Park in New York would be laid out in the same spirit—an enclave of romantic wilderness in the tight grip of a modern city.

At the same time, other eighteenth-century men were interested in Chi-nese philosophy. Two ideas, especially, appealed to the rationalist Western mind: the Confucian dislike of supernaturalism, and Confucian stress on the arts of government. Voltaire considered that "their empire is in truth the best the world has ever seen." He continued, ". . . its government the best possible and longest established, its morality the loftiest and most beautiful, its laws, its policy, its art, its industry . . . a model for all nations of the earth."

But the passion was one-sided. In 1793, the Chinese Emperor Ch'ien Lung dismissed an English ambassador assigned to work out trade agreements between the two countries. "The Celestial Empire," stated Ch'ien Lung in his mandate to Lord Macartney, "ruling all within the four seas . . . has not the slightest need of your country's manufacture." By the nineteenth cen-tury, Chinese standoffishness and complicated political and psychological stresses in the West bred a reaction, and the lighthearted ferment of Chinoiserie dissipated itself in the somber new world of revolution and machine industry.

The next travelers to the East were Protestant missionaries and, ironically, their companions in time, the merchants of the opium trade. While one group labored to save the heathen souls, the other helped undermine much of the physical energy of the Chinese and the economic health of the Empire. In 1850, an uprising of fanatic Chinese Christians resulted in the burning and looting of Buddhist and Confucian temples. A decade later, British and French troops burned the Summer Palace in Peking to punish the Manchus for exterminating a party of Western envoys. At the turn of the century, the last Manchu empress, Tz'u-hsi, unleashed her pugnacious anti-Western Society of the Harmonious Fist. The Boxer Rebellion was crushed by Western troops, and the rest of the twentieth century to date has been marked by crises of violence.

And yet some hope for understanding and tangible steps in that direction could be seen on both sides. The burning of the Summer Palace released a flood of pent-up works of art that, finding their way into collections in London, Paris, Berlin and the United States, stimulated new popular and scholarly interest in China. Archaeology, in the second decade of the century, proceeded fruitfully, as did the translation of historical documents. By now, three generations of China scholars have emerged in the West, in spite of two World Wars and the Chinese Civil War, which again destroyed her links with the West.

Mao Tse-tung, who came out on top after the Chinese Civil War, has taken pains to adapt his teachings to ancient doctrines, while bending them to achieve his own ends. "There cannot be two suns in one sky," he says, assuming the position of the Son of Heaven, whose religious trappings he has, however, dispensed with. In order to set his young people free to transform the society of their elders, he has attacked the Confucian teaching of filial loyalty. But he has substituted another abstraction for "the past," which is "the party," an overriding concept toward which young Maoists are induced to feel unquestioning loyalty. He has tried to demolish the reputation of the haughty "white cranes," those unworldly scholars who even in T'ang times worried the government by their refusal to join in an active life. "What is the most precious thing on earth?" asks Mao. "It is Man . . . our people are poor and blank, but the most beautiful poem can be written on a blank sheet of paper." And so he invokes the Taoist poet.

134

All men, the Chinese believe, are equal, which is to say they are born equally endowed with minds which can be molded into the "right" way of thinking. That principle does not, however, necessarily lead to the next logical one: that men deserve equal treatment before law or by each other. That is a conclusion which has been put forward in the West.

And yet, as we have seen, conflicting schools taught side by side in the past in China. Buddhist temples in Ch'ang-an cast their shadows not far from the crossroads where Manichean and Confucian ones stood. The Central Kingdom, we remember, has not always been forbidden territory and Westerners may well travel the routes of Hsüan-tsang and Marco Polo again one day. There are footpaths along the hills, wrote Mencius. "If suddenly they be used, they become roads."

Then, however, he went on to warn that, "if as suddenly they are not used, the wild grass fills them up."

Comparative History Chart

Dynasty	Some Events in China	Parallel Events in West
SHANG C.1523–1027 B.C.		Pharoah Ramses II 1292–1225 B.C. Trojan War c.1184 B.C.
CHOU C.1027–256 B.C. Western Chou c. 771 B.C. Spring and Autumn 722–481 B.C. Warring States 403–221 B.C.	Lao-tzu c.604–529 B.C. Confucius c.551–472 B.C. Mencius 372–289 B.C.	Buddha in India c.566– 480 B.C. Founding of Rome 509 B.C. Battle of Marathon 490 B.C. Plato 427–347 B.C. Alexander the Great 356–323 B.C.
CH'IN 221–206 B.C.	Great Wall "Burning of the Books"	2nd Punic War 218–201 B.C.
HAN 206 B.C.-A.D. 220 Former Han 206 B.C.-A.D. 9 Hsin 9–23 A.D. Later Han 25–220	Wu-Ti 157 B.C. Ming-Ti 58–75 A.D. Introduction of Buddhism	Contact with Rome Birth of Jesus c.8–4 B.C. Roman Empire—Augustus 31 B.C.-A.D. 14
THREE KINGDOMS Shu 221–263 (South- west) Wei 220–265 (North) Wu 222–280 (South- east)		
WESTERN CHIN 265–316 EASTERN CHIN 317–420	Dynastic power in south Confusion in north	Constantine adopts Chris- tianity 313 Establishes Constantinople 330
SOUTHERN and 420–589 NORTHERN DYNASTIES 386– 581 Northern Wei 386–535	Great Buddhist flowering	Fall of Rome to Vandals 401 Dark Ages begin

SUI 589–618	Reunification Grand Canal	
T'ANG 618–906	Kao-tsu 618–626 T'ai Tsung 627–649 Empress Wu 684–704 Ming Huang 712–756 An Lu-shan's revolt 755 Buddhist persecution 844	Mohammad 570–632 Islam conquers Spain 711–713 Charlemagne 768–814 Alfred the Great 871–899
FIVE DYNASTIES 907–960	Confusion throughout China	
SUNG 960–1279 North Sung 960–1126 South Sung 1127–1279	Fall of Kaifeng to Kin 1126 Rise of Mongols Genghis Khan	Romanesque revival 11– 12th centuries Crusades 11–13th centuries Gothic Era 13–14th centuries
YÜAN 1279–1368	Mongol rule Kublai Khan 1280	Marco Polo to Peking 1275
MING 1368–1644	Portuguese in Canton 1517 Father Ricci to Peking 1601 English in Canton 1637	Renaissance in Italy 15th century Gutenberg printing press 1436 Age of Exploration 16th century
CH'ING 1644–1912	Opium War 1839–1842 Christian Missionaries in China from U.S. and Europe 19th century Boxer Rebellion 1900	Declaration of Independ- ence 1776 French Revolution 1789
REPUBLIC 1912– PEOPLE'S REPUBLIC 1949–		

Further Reading List

The following books have been included for additional relatively simple, reading. Some of them, like Professor Needham's monumental four volumes, are obviously over the heads of most young people. But even a short time spent turning the pages of these volumes should give an idea of how exciting a field lies ahead for future China scholars.

Andersson, J. Gunnar. *Children of the Yellow Earth* (K. Paul, Trench, Trubner & Co. 1934)

Bible of the World. Robert O. Ballou, ed. (Viking Press, N. Y. 1939)

Cahill, James. *Chinese Painting* (Skira, N. Y. 1960)

Cohen, Joan L. *Buddha* (Delacorte, N. Y. 1969)

Crump, James & Irving. *Dragon Bones in the Yellow Earth* (Dodd Mead, N. Y. 1963)

From the Chinese. R. C. Trevelyan, ed. (Oxford, London. 1945)

Honour, Hugh. *Chinoiserie, the Vision of Cathay* (John Murray, London. 1961)

The Jade Mountain. Witter Bynner, tr. (Doubleday Anchor, N. Y. 1964)

Lee, Sherman. *A History of Far Eastern Art* (Abrams, N. Y. 1964)

The Legacy of China. R. Dawson, ed. (Oxford. Clarendon Press. 1964)

Needham, Joseph. *Science and Civilization in China* (Cambridge University Press, N. Y. 1961)

Reischauer, Edwin O. *Ennin's Diary* (Roland Press, N. Y. 1955)

Schafer, Edward H. *Golden Peaches of Samarkand* (Berkeley. 1963)
        The Vermillion Bird (Berkeley. 1967)

Stein, Sir Mark Aurel. *Ruins of Desert Cathay* (Macmillan, London. 1912)
    On Central Asian Tracks. Jeanette Mirsky, ed. (Pantheon, N. Y. 1964)

Travels of Marco Polo (Orion Press, N. Y.)

Waley, Arthur. *Ballads and Stories from Tun Huang* (Allen & Unwin, London. 1960)
        Li Po (Allen and Unwin. 1950)
        Po Chu-I (Allen & Unwin. 1949)
        The Real Tripitaka (Allen & Unwin. 1952)

The White Pony. Robert Payne, tr. (Mentor, N. Y., John Day, N. Y. 1947)

Wright, A. F. "Ch'ang-an" in *Cities of Destiny*. A. Toynbee, ed. (McGraw Hill, N. Y. 1967)

Wu Ch'eng-en. *Monkey*. Arthur Waley, tr. (Grove Press, N. Y. 1958)

A number of these have given permission to reprint, for which we are deeply grateful.